DRAMATIC ACTS

A Guidebook to Making Meaning in the Theatre

Colleen Reilly, Editor
Deb Cohen
Rebecca Morrice
Gordon Phetteplace
David Skeele
Laura Smiley
Slippery Rock University

Kendall Hunt
publishing company

Cover image © *'Tis Pity She's a Whore*, directed by David Skeele for the Slippery Rock University Department of Theatre, 2005

Kendall Hunt
publishing company

www.kendallhunt.com
Send all inquiries to:
4050 Westmark Drive
Dubuque, IA 52004-1840

Copyright © 2012 by Deb Cohen, Rebecca Morrice, Gordon Phetteplace, Colleen Reilly, David Skeele, and Laura Smiley

ISBN 978-1-4652-0187-4

Printed in the United States of America
10 9 8 7 6 5 4 3 2 1

CONTENTS

SCOPE AND SEQUENCE

The objective of this text is to provide an introduction to the definitions, processes, and styles of theatre. Theatre is a medium of expression that has many meanings for multiple cultures, communities, and historical contexts. It is also a professional industry that contributes to the economic, social, and artistic climate of contemporary society. This text will outline the methodologies of Attending and Making theatre as it relates to you as an undergraduate in a liberal arts curriculum, a member of a campus community that celebrates the arts, and a citizen of the world.

The study of theatre at Slippery Rock University is focused on providing an understanding of its vital and necessary role in any society. Throughout this text we will examine the process of making meaning in the theatre. We will explore the strategies through which theatre practitioners communicate their vision. To achieve this we must look back at historical theatrical movements as we look forward to emerging theatrical practices. Our inquiry will be guided by the scholarly and professional experiences of the SRU theatre faculty and their collaborators.

ABOUT THE AUTHORS

Deb Cohen, PhD, teaches Spanish language and Hispanic cultures at Slippery Rock University. She has published articles on Latin American theatre in *TDR (The Drama Review)* and the *Latin American Theatre Review*. Cohen has translated a number of Latin American plays, including *Only You, Chapulines and Other Critters*, and *The Man Who Turned Into a Dog*, which she directed at SRU. In addition, her translation of Melvin Méndez's *The Old Man's Wings* was staged in 2009 by the SRU theatre department. In her spare time, "Dr. Deb" takes theatre classes in design and tech, and paints sets for SRU productions.

Rebecca Morrice, MFA, received her BA in History of Art and Architecture from the University of Illinois at Chicago, and her MFA in costume design from the University of Illinois at Urbana-Champaign. She has designed costumes for theatre, dance, and opera, and has worked with a wide variety of theatre companies including American Players Theatre, CENTERSTAGE in Baltimore, Illinois Repertory Theatre, Geva Theatre, and Unseam'd Shakespeare. She is currently a member of the faculty at Slippery Rock University where she teaches costume design and technology, stage makeup, theatrical design history, and stage management.

Colleen Reilly, PhD, MLIS, MA: Since 1991 Colleen has served as an Arts Educator, Arts Administrator, Company Manager, Stage Manager, and Dramaturg for numerous organizations including Charleston Stage Company, the Spoleto Festival U.S.A., Children's Theatre of Charlotte, Opera Carolina, Pandora's Box, and Theatre 99. Each year she serves as the Festival Manager for the Piccolo Spoleto Fringe Festival at Theatre 99, which sees as many as 10,000 patrons in 16 days. She holds a PhD in Theatre History and Performance Studies from the University of Pittsburgh, where she also earned an MLIS in Archival Studies. She serves on the Executive Board of the Theatre Library Association, and has archived collections from the Yale School of Drama and the Historic Pittsburgh Project. She teaches classes in theatre history and dramatic literature, and leads the curriculum in Arts Administration at Slippery Rock University where she also serves as the Director of the Kaleidoscope Arts Festival.

David Skeele, PhD, MFA, MA, teaches playwriting and acting and directs productions at Slippery Rock University. His SRU productions include *Tallgrass Gothic, Jesus Christ Superstar, Cymbeline, Hedda Gabler, Pericles,* and *'Tis Pity She's a Whore*. David's original plays have received professional and collegiate productions in Los Angeles, Pittsburgh, Cleveland, Columbus, Omaha, and Orlando. Recently, SRU produced several of David's plays of supernatural horror—*Dark North, The Margins,* and *Deepchurch Hollow*—and brought them to the Edinburgh Festival Fringe in Edinburgh, Scotland, where they each received coveted five-star reviews. His horror novel *Raised In Darkness* is available on Kindle from amazon.com.

Laura Smiley, MFA, is an associate professor of theatre at Slippery Rock University. She teaches a variety of performance classes including Fundamentals of Acting, Directing, Auditioning Technique, Voice and Movement, and Acting Shakespeare. She has directed numerous performances for Slippery Rock Theatre, including *Fat Pig,* which was invited to perform at the American College Theatre Festival in 2011, and *Deepchurch Hollow,* which performed at the Edinburgh Fringe Festival, Scotland in 2010. Other recent SRU projects include *The 25th Annual Putnam County Spelling Bee, The Old Man's Wings, Inspecting Carol, Cabaret,* and *As You Like It.* Smiley is the artistic and executive director of the Unseam'd Shakespeare Company which she founded in 1994. Along with acting and directing in the Pittsburgh area, she has taught acting, voice, and movement at many area universities, including Point Park University, the University of Pittsburgh, and the Indiana University of Pennsylvania. In addition to many roles with Unseam'd Shakespeare, Laura has performed for the Pittsburgh Public Theatre, City Theatre, Starlight Productions, and her one-woman show, *Building.* She has guest directed for Living Images Arts in NYC, Bloomsburg University, and Indiana University of Pennsylvania, as well as for collaborations with the City Theatre and the Pittsburgh Chamber Music Society. She received her BFA in Acting from the Catholic University of America, Washington, DC, and her MFA in Acting from the University of Pittsburgh. She is a member in good standing in AEA, SAG, AFTRA, and the SAFD.

ATTENDING THEATRE

Colleen Reilly

Theatre is an art form that occurs under the unlikeliest of circumstances, and yet it has been practiced since the earliest formations of civilization. In its most basic formation, theatre requires the creation and presentation of an action in the presence of an audience collected in a particular space. There are four fundamental elements of theatre.

1	PRACTITIONER	A theatre PRACTITIONER is anyone who contributes to the making of theatrical art. As a fundamental unit of theatre, the PRACTITIONER refers to the presence of a live performer presenting an action.
2	ACTION	Aristotle defined drama as the "imitation of an action." As a fundamental unit of theatre the ACTION refers to that which is being dramatized or performed; i.e., what is the PRACTITIONER doing?
3	THEATRE	As a fundamental unit of theatre, the term "THEATRE" refers to the space in which the PRACTITIONER presents the ACTION. The THEATRE may be a traditional performance space or a space adapted for performance.
4	AUDIENCE	The presence of the AUDIENCE is the defining feature of theatrical art. The "liveness" of the theatrical event is what distinguishes it from other art forms.

Simply stated, for theatre to occur a PRACTITIONER must perform an ACTION in a THEATRE in the presence of an AUDIENCE.

Theatre practitioners will be discussed at length in the next section of the text, "Making Theatre." While many of you may be interested in the craft of the theatre, here we will discuss the role of the public sector in theatre arts through a discussion of Audiences, Theatre Spaces, and Performing Arts Organizations. Who is in the audience? What trends impact audience participation in the arts? Where do we attend theatre? How do these spaces inform theatre experiences? Who provides the resources to support theatre as an art form? We will explore these questions, create a common vocabulary, and invite you to think of the social implications of theatre in your communities.

THEATRE AUDIENCES

Colleen Reilly

CHAPTER OBJECTIVES

- To recognize theatre as a social transaction between practitioners and audiences.
- To cite the factors that contribute to active and passive audiences.
- To define aesthetic distance and consider its relationship to theatre.
- To understand the expectations of theatre etiquette.
- To define audience development and to understand many of its challenges.

I want to begin by considering the role of the audience in the process of making meaning in the theatre. If we think of "theatre" as a cycle of choices being made by playwrights, directors, designers, actors, and producers, we can think of the audience as the conduit for that cycle. Theatre is by nature a social transaction. As American filmmaker, actor, theatre director, and screenwriter Orson Welles once said, "I want to give the audience a hint of a scene. No more than that. Give them too much and they won't contribute anything themselves. Give them a suggestion and you get them working with you. That's what gives the theatre meaning: when it becomes a social act." (Collier's, 29 January 1938.)

The social act of theatre is what makes it stand apart from other art forms. The presence of the audience is the defining feature of theatrical art. The social transaction of theatre cannot occur without an audience. The word "audience" means several different things, such as (1) a group of spectators at a public event, and (2) the *act* of hearing or attending to words and sounds. Let's take a moment to consider this distinction. In the first description the audience is a passive collective of individuals who are required to observe an event. The second description refers to an active process of engagement. The tension between an active and passive audience defines current trends in studying audience behavior.

Whether dealing with an active or passive audience situation, theatre practitioners will agree that there is a certain element of theatre that is crucial to its success but yet is invisible. **Synergy**, being a combination of the words *energy* and *synthesis*, is a type of energy that is shared between the audience and the performers. Without it, the performance would be flat and the audience would be uninvolved. Consider a performance of any type that you may have given (even playing on a sports team counts here!) and try to recall how the audience's reactions may have either helped or hindered you. If your audience was supportive and attentive, you were probably well aware of that and it helped you in your effort. However, if they were distracted and uninterested, as a performer, that was probably a bit daunting. Theatre practitioners of all types actively try to cultivate a strong sense of **synergy** in their work.

–Rebecca Morrice

Active Audiences

Historically, audiences have much more actively participated in the social transaction of theatre. We can trace the origins of the theatre that we practice to fifth-century BC Greece where part of the civic identity of the populace was defined by their attendance at and participation in an annual playwriting competition. Citizens actually campaigned to be elected as judges for the dramatic contest, and were vocal about their opinions about the performance. The audience comprised all levels of the social order from state and religious officials to possibly women and slaves, although scholars debate their participation. Everyone gathered for the communal religious and civic celebration of dramatic art. It transpired in the course of the day, and had a festival atmosphere that is sometimes forgotten in the solemn presentation of classical dramatic texts.

Roman audiences attended theatre alongside a wide spectrum of entertainments including mock battles, horse racing, exotic animal expositions and competitions, and generalized spectacles of violence. There is no evidence to suggest that their behavior was modified when faced with theatrical entertainments. In fact, it would appear that Roman practitioners faced many of the challenges of active audiences in what may be the first example of suggested theatre etiquette.

From the Prologue to playwright Plautus's *Poenulus* circa 210 BC: *Let no worn out harlot sit in front of the stage ... nor the usher roam about in front of people or show anyone to a seat while the actor is on the stage. Those who have had a leisurely nap at home should now cheerfully stand, or at least refrain from sleeping. Keep slaves from occupying the seats, there will be room for free men ... And let the nurses keep tiny children at home and not bring them to see the play ... Let matrons view the play in silence, laugh in silence, refrain from tinkling tones of chatter, they should take home their gossip...*

The Elizabethan public theatres where Shakespeare staged many of his plays in the sixteenth and seventeenth centuries were also festive environments. Theatrical presentations competed for audiences with cockfighting, bearbaiting, and other entertainments. Many of these occurred simultaneously just beyond the exterior of the outdoor playhouses. Inside these theatres patrons' admission could be gained for as little as a penny, but additional amenities such as a seat with a cushion or in a private box were as much as six times that amount.

BOX OFFICE

The box office is the location for ticket sales. The terms derive from Elizabethan public theatres where patrons dropped their pennies in a centrally located box which was then stored in an office offstage during the performance—thus the title "Box Office." Most contemporary theatres offer phone and online sales in addition to regular box office hours. Many times you must purchase your tickets directly at the box office in order to receive any discounts.

Nearly one third of the Elizabethan audience stood throughout the performance, and there is evidence that gambling, trading, thievery, and prostitution were rampant in the public theatres while the play progressed.

GROUNDLING

A spectator who stood in the yard or pit of Elizabethan public theatres. The term became slang for people of unsophisticated taste. In 1964 a comedy improvisation troupe in Los Angeles took the name and since has launched the careers of comedians like Will Ferrell, Lisa Kudrow, Kathy Griffin, and countless others.

French and Italian theatres of the Renaissance were equally divided between the entertainment on the stage and that provided by the audience interacting with the performance. While most plays were produced indoors, audience seating extended to chairs placed on the stage that could be purchased by the aristocracy.

This continued into the eighteenth century when theatre architecture emphasized the class divisions with seating available in the pit, gallery, and box. It is important to note, however, that none of the seating was fixed to the floor. Seats could be moved to accommodate a view of the stage or other audience members.

The experience that many of us take for granted in the theatre of assigned seating and darkened auditoriums is a relatively "new" way for audiences to interact with the stage. As recently as 100 years ago most theatres contained no *house lights* or controlled lighting for the audience. Audiences shared the illumination from the stage, and were active, sometimes to the point of being rowdy. They commented on what they were seeing to each other and to the performers on stage. They freely demanded that actors repeat **soliloquies**, and other poetic forms of dramatic texts. As in the definition of *audience*, they were engaged in the act of hearing and attending to words and had very high expectations for the performers.

SOLILOQUY

A dramatic speech through which a character reveals his or her inner thoughts and emotions. The most famous soliloquies are found in Shakespeare, such as Hamlet's *To Be or Not to Be*.

Audience seating on benches or free standing chairs could be rearranged at will. Tickets allowed patrons to gain entry to the performance, but did not require them to sit still or be quiet. If there was something occurring on stage that did not meet their standards, they would sometimes shout the performers off stage. Their evaluation of the performance ranged from expectations to how certain language should be delivered to the preference for a particular actor, much in the same way that we follow celebrities in the media and patronize their films, music, and Facebook pages.

My favorite example of audience behavior in the nineteenth century is the 1849 Astor Place Riot. Tensions were high in the Astor Opera House as English actor William Charles Macready took the stage for a performance of *Macbeth* on May 7, 1849. The top level of seating had been purchased by hundreds of supporters of actor Edwin Forrest, Macready's American rival. Macready was shouted off the stage after a barrage of rotten eggs, potatoes, and sundry other items greeted his entrance. He vowed to return to the more civilized stages of England but was persuaded to deliver a second performance on May 10. The militia was called to police the 10,000 people who arrived at the theatre to take sides on the Forrest-Macready divide. The crowd broke into violence and 22 people were killed.

While there are many factors that contributed to the escalation to violence over an acting quarrel—such as class warfare, friction between English and American cultural identities, and divisions across political parties—the reality that this quarrel took place in the theatre speaks to the dynamic cultural space that theatre occupied in the nineteenth century. We tend to think of the theatre now as a place for our most polite and formal behavior, but our roots as a national culture are embedded in a much more relaxed and democratized space.

Passive Audiences

How did we move from the pub-like atmosphere of the nineteenth century to the church-like theatre of the twenty-first? Two inventions of the twentieth century contributed directly to aligning theatergoers to the first definition of *audience* as a group of spectators at a public event.

1. **CONTROLLED LIGHTING**
2. **THE INTRODUCTION OF THEATRE ETIQUETTE**

Controlled Lighting

At the turn of the twentieth century theatres radically altered the theatergoing experience by making the transition from gas lamps to electrical lighting. Not only did this eliminate the noxious fumes that would have permeated the **house**, but also practitioners were able to begin to control audience behavior by dimming the lights over the audience and more brightly illuminating the stage.

HOUSE
The seating area for the audience. This term can also refer to the seating capacity and arrangement; i.e., how many seats in the house tonight? Or, the house is empty. The lobby or reception area is referred to as the Front of House and is staffed by personnel who coordinate with other theatre practitioners to facilitate the audience experience. These include the Box Office Manager, Box Office Staff, House Manager, and Ushers.

Audiences who were accustomed to seeing and being seen were guided toward a more passive experience of observation. Furthermore, the experience of sitting in the dark discouraged audience participation and conversation, making the theatre experience more personal and private.

Changes in the lighting of the house also contributed to more control of **aesthetic distance** for practitioners of theatre. Aesthetic distance is a strategy used by practitioners to affect an audience's emotional identification with the world of the play. Some performances demand that the audience become completely absorbed and invested in the circumstances of the play, in which case there is little aesthetic distance between the audience and the performance. Other performances require that the audience remain objective and aware that the circumstances of the play are radically different from their own reality. In this case there is extreme aesthetic distance.

When I saw *August: Osage County* on Broadway, I was completely drawn into the story and lives of the characters of this domestic drama. The play was three hours long but when the lights came up for intermission, I just wanted to see what happened next. This is an example of little aesthetic distance. When I go experience a Cirque du Soleil production, there is a magical world created that I am drawn to, but the experience is so extraordinary and full of spectacle that I am always reminded that I am watching a performance, one that I also enjoy. This is an example of great aesthetic distance.

–Laura Smiley

Another way to think of aesthetic distance is to ask yourself: to what extent am I being asked to believe the events I am watching are real? To what extent am I being reminded that I am watching a performance of something?

AESTHETIC DISTANCE

The degree of emotional connection or identification with a performance. Little aesthetic distance means that the audience feels very close and is absorbed in the world of the play. Great aesthetic distance means that the audience remains aware of a performance and/or is constantly reminded that the world of the play is a fictional construction.

The Introduction of Theatre Etiquette

Many of you may have had your first theatergoing experience through a school field trip to a matinee performance. It is likely that in preparation for this experience you were instructed by your teacher how to behave in the theatre, or at the very least, handed a program note or leaflet that outlined the expectations of your behavior. The development of **theatre etiquette** has had a profound effect on audience behavior since its introduction in the early twentieth century.

THEATRE ETIQUETTE

A system of prescribed behavior determined by cultural organizations to facilitate a positive experience for artists and audience members.

Scholars mark a shift in divisions between "Arts" and "Entertainment" in the turn of the twentieth century that corresponds with increasing class consciousness. They argue that the monied classes claimed the Arts, and left Entertainment to the rest of us. In order to regain access to the Arts we were asked to model the behavior of the upper classes, who prescribed a new relationship to attending performances. The active audience was silenced, and the relationship between performances and audiences became more and more reverential.

Over time theatre etiquette has become more relaxed, and faced new challenges as audiences have recommitted themselves to active participation. For many people that includes engaging with social media at all times to enhance and record their experience. However, it remains inappropriate to text, tweet, or update your Facebook status during a performance. This is not only a matter of etiquette, but also one of controlled lighting! Surveys reveal that the backlighting of electronic devices in a dark house is the single most cited distraction for audience and performers alike.

SLIPPERY ROCK UNIVERSITY THEATRE ETIQUETTE

While attending our performances we want you to relax, enjoy, and be yourselves. We also want to safeguard the experience for other patrons and for the many people who have worked hard to make this production a success. We recommend the following to optimize your experience:

1. Arrive on time. Late seating can be problematic due to lighting and safety concerns. It can also be a distraction to other audience members and the performers. In the event that you do arrive late, please cooperate with our house manager who will seat you at the first designated opportunity!
2. Turn off electronic devices. The sound and lighting can be distracting and/or dangerous to actors making entrances and exits under extremely dark conditions. The electronic signal can also interfere with our wireless technology and disrupt our technical processes.
3. Do not take photographs or use recording devices. We are bound by copyright law to protect the integrity of this performance and cannot allow unauthorized reproductions.
4. Complete the social transaction. Voice your responses after the performance through social media, community forums, and publications. Attend talkbacks, contact our department, and become involved.

Contemporary Theatre Audiences

The key to your participation at theatre events is to discover where your preference for audience participation falls on the spectrum between active and passive. There is no one-size-fits-all solution, but by accumulating audience experiences you will develop a better perspective on what kinds of performances you might enjoy. Theatre does not exist as a monolithic institution, and comes in many forms. In addition to the performances that you will be attending this semester, consider the following:

IF YOU LIKE:	THEN YOU COULD TRY:
Interacting with performers Commenting on performances	Improvisational Theatre
Spectacle Familiar story lines or songs	Musical Theatre
A relaxed atmosphere Dining during the performance	Shakespeare in the Park

Audience development has become an important consideration for many practitioners seeking to build, enhance, or attract individuals to participate in arts events. Professionals working in audience development identify barriers to attendance for potential audiences and address them by creating new points of entry, or ways that audiences can access arts experiences. Barriers to attendance can include, cost, location, and attitudes towards the arts.

AUDIENCE DEVELOPMENT

The goals of audience development are increasing awareness of, and participation in, the activities of arts organizations. Effective audience development is incorporated into the full range of an organization's activities, including programming, operations, marketing and public relations, education and outreach, and fund-raising.

The cost of tickets is often a barrier to attendance for many potential audience members, but there are ways to negotiate individual ticket prices. You can take advantage of volunteer programs, student discounts, or subscription packages.

THEATRE TICKETS

1. Volunteer: Many arts organizations, including the Slippery Rock Theatre Department, offer free seating to performances for which you volunteer to usher or assist with the front of house.
2. Single Ticket Purchases: Look for ongoing student discounts, or "rush" specials that allow you to purchase tickets at special prices on the day of the performance.
3. Subscriptions: You can sometimes save considerable money over single ticket purchases by becoming a subscriber, which means buying a package or "subscription" that includes tickets to several or all of a theatre's productions during a season. Many theatres offer "Flex Tickets" where you purchase a pre-selected number of tickets in advance, and can use them for any production of that theatre in the season, or within a designated time period.

Many theatres fail to attract new audiences because they do not extend themselves to a large enough geographic area. Where there is a high concentration of theatrical activity, in New York, Philadelphia, Chicago, London, and Los Angeles, for example, theatre districts emerge as destinations for locals and tourists alike to participate in arts experiences. They draw audiences large enough to sustain their theatrical activity. Cultural districts are often formed in areas where there may be the presence of multiple arts organizations, but less theatrical activity. Pittsburgh has a cultural district.

The Cultural District is home to Downtown Pittsburgh's dynamic art and entertainment scene. Discover a plethora of choices for live entertainment—contemporary music, modern dance, visual art and thought-provoking theatre, as well as classical music, opera, ballet, popular musical theatre, and more. http://www.culturaldistrict.org/

Cultural districts can reconcile location and attitudes towards the arts. The formation of cultural districts is often part of a larger process of urban renewal and revitalization. As residents are able to reclaim part of their urban landscape through theatres, galleries, and restaurants, they begin to experience the value of the arts in their communities. Cultural districts also allow organizations to share resources and audiences. They provide a kind of "one-stop shopping" for people looking for arts experiences.

Attitudes towards the arts are one of the largest barriers to participation that audiences and practitioners face. Interest in and access to the arts is tied to economic cycles of growth and decline. In periods of economic boom, consumers extend their largesse to arts participation and philanthropy. In periods of economic restraint, the institution of theatre faces debates over its value to society.

That perceived value is complicated by emerging forms of arts participation including live broadcast of performances to satellite locations, access to productions via social media, trends in personalized arts experiences through emerging technologies, and distribution of theatrical performances through 3-D movies. Practitioners in the theatre are exploring new methods to ensure the social transaction of the live event.

Human beings have gathered to share stories in every known society, and in its broadest definition we can see theatrical practice in every historical epoch. Over time theatre has served as a religious ritual, a political tool, a form of protest, and a celebration of humanity. We tend to think of these modes of performance as being disparate, but they often overlap. For today's society, theatre can mean many different things such as a physical space, a form of art and/or entertainment, and something tourists like to see in big cities.

The question, "Why attend the theatre?" is one that scholars, critics, and practitioners share with the theatergoing and non-theatergoing public alike. Historically, the practice of theatre has been a central function of civic life. The word "theatre" derives from the Greek expression *theatron* or "seeing place". For classical civilization, the theatre provided a public space to see, be seen, and to present dramatic action. Today theatre exists on the margins of many other "seeing" activities, including film, television, and social media. The next chapter will more deeply investigate the "seeing places" of theatre spaces.

Conclusion

Theatre is a social transaction that can only occur in the presence of the audience. Historically, the nature of that transaction has been extremely active as compared to the more passive role prescribed to today's audiences. Aesthetic distance plays a role in guiding audience behavior, as does training in theatre etiquette and traditional audience experiences. Audience development seeks not only to attract more audience members but also to create more active audience experiences. These practices emphasize the role of the audience in making meaning in the theatre.

Suggested Exercises

Obtain prior approval to attend a performance in addition to the two productions assigned. Prepare a 1-2 page description of the production that you attend that must contain the following. (Hint: Try to use language more specific than "good" or "bad.")

- Name of Play, Theatre, and Location
- Paragraph 1: A thesis statement that describes the idea of the play, or what you think it is about. No synopsis!
- Paragraph 2: Describe the choices made by the director, actors, and designers. Do they work? Why, or why not?
- Paragraph 3: Describe a scene from the play that supports your thesis statement and evaluation of the effectiveness of the theatrical choices. Make a conclusive statement.

THEATRE SPACES

Rebecca Morrice

CHAPTER OBJECTIVES

- Identify different types of theatre spaces such as arena, proscenium, and thrust.
- List features of theatre spaces from different historical periods.
- Trace the development of scenery through different historical periods.
- Recognize that different styles of theatre require different spaces.
- Locate current theatre architecture as a relatively new development in theatre history.

Like many elements within our modern culture, the *building* you most likely occupy when attending your theatre course owes a great debt to the cultures that came before. Of the styles of theatre building common to the modern cultures of the Western Hemisphere (primarily the Americas and Western Europe), many elements can be traced all the way back to the ancient Greeks in the fifth and sixth centuries BC. Other elements were introduced during the medieval and Renaissance eras. In essence a modern theatre space is an interesting medley of ideas that have been forged together over time, most of which have been chosen specifically with the best interests of the audience—you—in mind.

> Look around a modern theatre building. What are some of the elements that you can recognize as being common to many modern theatres? Is it an *arena* theatre or *theatre in the round?* Is the stage raised up? Is there an area in front of the raised stage where an *orchestra* might be seated? Are the seats placed at an angle or *rake?* The Greeks were doing all of this at least two thousand years ago. Is there a curtain? The ancient Romans first did that. Is it a *proscenium* style theatre? Is there painted *perspective scenery?* Is the theatre indoors? These are all elements that were first introduced during the Renaissance, five to six hundred years ago.

Types of Theatre Spaces

We'll begin this section by introducing some of the most common types of spaces used in Western theatre today.

Arena theatre (aka *theatre in the round)* is a theatre space in which the audience surrounds the acting/performance space. This type of stage space usually allows the audience to sit closer to the action, but cannot make use of a lot of scenery because it would block the audience's view.

Proscenium theatre is a space in which the audience faces the acting/ performance space and is usually separated from the actors by a *proscenium arch* which acts like a picture frame. This is the style of theatre space most familiar to audiences today. Is it also referred to as *theatre of the fourth-wall removed* because it reflects how watching a performance in this style is often like watching the characters inside a box that has had one side removed. It allows us to voyeuristically peer into their world—seemingly without them knowing we are watching!

Thrust theatre is a space in which the audience sits on three sides of the acting/performance space. This type of theatre space combines elements of the previous two, in that the three sided seating allows the audience to sit closer to the stage then they would in a proscenium style theatre and allows for more scenery than there could be in an arena format. For many modern directors, this style of theatre space is quite desirable in that it offers "the best of both worlds."

Other types of theatre spaces that you might experience as an audience member include:

Alley theatre which is a space that places a long narrow stage in between two long banks of seating. **Think of it almost like a tennis court with seating on either side of the playing space.**

—**Laura Smiley**

Environmental space, which has nothing to do necessarily with the outdoors, but instead is a type of theatre where the boundaries between where the audience exists and where the performers exist are blurred.

Found space, refers to a space that is not ordinarily a theatre, which was chosen for the performance because it provides the perfect location as it already is. **Quantum Theatre in Pittsburgh exclusively creates productions in found spaces. I saw *The Crucible* performed in the Rose Garden at Mellon Park. Director Roger Henderson says, "I wanted to explore the idea that nature has gone awry…and that not having walls does not prevent them from trapping themselves." There were wooden platforms built in various places in the Garden, surrounded by overgrown hedges and weeds; this for me signified how difficult it is to restrain nature.**

—**Laura Smiley**

A *black-box theatre* is an indoor space (it can be anything!) that is often painted black and has flexible seating and lighting positions. This type of theatre can be rearranged to create whatever configuration of space is best for the current production.

Historically, it is said that the first theatre spaces were *arena* or *theatre-in-the-round* spaces. Some say this is because humans are compelled to form circles, but really, the reason is much more simple. When there is something that a group of people want to see, the most logical way to approach that situation is to surround the thing you want to see—and this includes a performance. There is nothing more psychological to it than the need to see what you want to see. Thus, the earliest stage spaces were *arena* because it was the most logical solution for the audience.

Ancient Greece

Before they began building permanent theatre spaces, the ancient Greeks were using *threshing circles* to perform in. These were circles of land outside of the towns that were cleared for the purpose of threshing grain.

These round spaces found a second purpose when they weren't in use for threshing—they became performance spaces. The performer(s) would stand in the center while the audience gathered in the circle around them to watch. Eventually these spaces were paved with stone and were called the **orchestra** or "playing place".

Once theatre gained a more important place within the religion and culture of Greece, they began to locate these orchestras at the base of natural hillsides which also gave the spaces great acoustics and let the people carve seating out of the hill itself. At first these benches were made out of wood, and later, out of stone. Many of these spaces, once built, were in continuous use for hundreds of years and still exist today.

Of all of the theatres built by the ancient Greeks, one of the best examples to study is the Theatre of Dionysus.

First built around the sixth century BC, the Theatre of Dionysus began as little more than a paved threshing circle with a nearby temple dedicated to the god Dionysus. Because much of the theatre created by the Ancient Greeks was directly connected to their polytheistic religion, their theatre spaces often had an altar, a temple, or both associated with them. This allowed the audience members not only to enjoy the entertainment, but also to pay their respects to the gods at the same time. In many ways, attending the theatre in the ancient Greek world was a little like attending church.

At first, the orchestra at the Theatre of Dionysus was perfectly circular with the audience surrounding on all sides. As the complexity of the plays performed there increased, the need for storage spaces for the masks and costumes commonly used increased as well. This led to the creation of a building called a **skene**, which was placed on one side of the orchestra and was one or two stories tall. This effectively changed the *arena* style theatre into a *thrust* format with the audience sitting around three sides of the orchestra in a seating area known as the *theatron* or *cavea*.

Though related to our word *scenery*, the *skene* building was not originally intended as scenery. In fact, the Greeks, whose outdoor theatre spaces were at the mercy of the weather, made little use of scenery as we think of it. Instead they relied

© 2012 Anastasios71. Under license from Shutterstock, Inc.

Example of an ancient Greek orchestra (dancing place).

© 2012 pryzmat. Under license from Shutterstock, Inc.

Another example of an ancient Greek orchestra (dancing place).

© National Geographic Society/Corbis

Orchestra and *skene* building with *pinakes* used as scenery.

on the words of the playwright, the actors, and the imagination of the audience to set the location of their plays.

Once the *skene* was built, it was only a short while before the idea of creating a raised stage occurred to the Greeks. This raised stage not only allowed the audience to see the actors better, but also introduced the idea of physical levels of performance to the Greek theatre. One of the conventions of the Greek theatre was the use of a *chorus*. The chorus was a group of performers (usually between eight and twelve) who spoke or chanted in unison during the play. In many ways, the chorus was meant to represent the audience who, if ever confused about what they should be thinking or feeling about the characters or ideas in the play, could look to the words of the chorus for guidance. As the plays developed, there became more of a desire or need to place the regular characters of the play on the raised stage while leaving the chorus to occupy the orchestra which was more physically connected to the audience. The idea of levels was even taken a step further when Greek playwrights began using the roofs of the *skene* buildings as locations where actors portraying the gods could perform. A crane-like machine was used to lift the god-actors into place on the roof and even led to the term **deus ex machina**, or literally, "god in the machine," which is a term we still use today to indicate a sudden and unexpected ending or outcome to a plot.

Eventually, a *skene* building, the *proskenion* which was a low platform between the *skene* and the orchestra, and a raised stage were added to the Theatre of Dionysus. These began to encroach on the orchestra causing it to become more of a semi-circle. In fact, as time progressed and the use of the chorus began to diminish, Greek theatres saw the orchestra as less and less important. It eventually became little more than a sliver of the circle it once had been. Modern theatres still retain this feature in the area in front of the raised stage where the group of musicians (the *orchestra*!) is seated when performing for musicals and operas.

While the Greeks did not use a great deal of scenery, the archaeological evidence from the theatres suggests to us that there were at least two devices that may have been used for this purpose.

The first were *pinakes,* which were flat panels that were inserted into grooves in the openings of some *skene* buildings. These were removeable and may have been used in a similar way to how modern theatre designers use *flats*. The other devices were *periaktoi,* whose purpose is still debated by historians. *Periaktoi* were stone prisms several feet tall with a hollowed center through which a pole could be placed. Several of these *periaktoi* were then lined up together. When all the *periaktoi* were turned to display any of their three faces, they worked similarly to modern moving billboards or like the letters used on the original version of the television program *Wheel of Fortune*. The mystery that still exists is what was painted on them. While the stones themselves have been found at these theatre sites, the paint that was on them has not survived time and the elements. It has been hypothesized that they may have been used as painted scenery. But, because they are found to the sides of the orchestra rather than behind, where scenery would traditionally be placed, the more plausible suggestion is that *periaktoi* were used as a playbill or program of sorts. Since many ancient Greek plays were presented as a part of a play competition, it is entirely possible that the *periaktoi* had the titles of plays and the names of playwrights painted on them. As the performance moved from play to play, the faces of

the *periaktoi* would be changed to keep the audience informed as to which play they were currently watching.

Ancient Rome

Ancient Roman theatres bear some strong resemblances to those of the ancient Greeks. In fact, many Roman theatres are actually remodeled Greek theatres. The Romans were well aware of the style of theatre space preferred by the Greeks and as they gradually became the predominant culture, they chose to adopt the Greek style of theatre but adapted it to better suit their needs. In the ancient Roman style of playwriting, the chorus was no longer an important element and, as such, the need for the orchestra diminished. In many Roman theatres, the orchestra was changed into seating for more privileged audience members. In others, the orchestra was surrounded by a barred-fence and animal fights were held there.

In Roman theatres, there became more of a focus on the building behind the raised stage.

While the Greeks called it *skene*, the Romans referred to it as a *scaenae frons* or *frons scaenae*—"scenic front"— which better reflects their more decorative approach to the building.

While still not exactly scenery in the modern sense the Roman theatre building has indeed become much more decorative with statues and columns covering

Ruins of an ancient Roman *scaenae frons*.

The Circus Maximus in Rome.

it. The Romans are also credited with creating the first stage curtain, the *aulaeum*, designed to keep scenic elements from the audience's view until a certain time. Unlike modern curtains, the *aulaeum* was usually lowered into a trough to reveal the view, rather than being raised out of the way.

The style of theatre architecture seen at the Theatre of Pompey in Rome was copied all over the Roman Empire. The Romans are well known historically for their advancements in engineering, which allowed them to build their theatres free-standing rather than carved out of hillsides. However, the people had more of a desire to watch gladiatorial combats and other types of entertainment than plays. To serve that desire, the Roman theatres often shared one wall of the building with another entertainment building known as a **circus**.

Circus buildings were built specifically for the purpose of chariot racing and had nothing at all to do with the modern definition of "circus." Instead these long narrow buildings were designed not only to house the thousands of spectators that would come to these popular events, but were also intentionally designed to cause spectacular crashes. For the Circus Maximus the center divider was angled, causing a bottleneck effect at the end of the track opposite the starting gate. As the incentive to win was very high for the competitors, the race became very dangerous and deadly, a detail the Roman spectators rather enjoyed.

Another unique type of theatre space that became popular for the Romans was the **amphitheatre** which is another example of *theatre in the round* where the audience surrounds the playing space. Perhaps most famous because of the well-known ruins of the Coliseum in Rome, the *amphitheatre* was a multipurpose entertainment space designed to showcase gladiatorial combats, exotic wild-animal fights, and **naumachiae**, or reenactments of sea battles.

Illustration of a Roman Chariot Race by C. Adamello.

Naumachiae (singular naumachia): From the Ancient Greek, literally means "naval combat." The first known naumachia was in fact given by Julius Caesar in Rome in 46 BC on the occasion of his quadruple triumph. He had a basin built next to the Tiber and made 2,000 combatants and 4,000 rowers, all prisoners of war, fight. Many lives were lost.

As the Roman empire expanded and battles were won, the Roman people had a desire to experience and celebrate the victories on the battlefields. *Amphitheatres* were designed with the capability to be flooded with water, allowing scale-model ships and hundreds to thousands of reenactors to replay the important moments from battles at sea. Without newspapers or television to keep them up-to-date, the Romans looked forward to these events to keep them informed. Unfortunately for many of the performers these reenactments were very realistic, and many people died while recreating the battles for entertainment.

Ruins of the Roman Flavian Amphitheatue, more commonly known as the Coliseum.

The Romans enjoyed their diversions and entertainments to the point that some historians cite this as a contributing cause of the Fall of Rome in 476 AD. Infighting among Roman citizens over favorite gladiators, and rampant absenteeism from jobs in favor of attending events, are cited as some of the possible causes for the demise of the Empire. The collapse of the Roman civilization was so devastating to the stability of the Western world that historians refer to the following time period as the Dark Ages (the fifth through the eighth centuries AD).

The Dark Ages

During the Dark Ages, theatre did not necessarily cease being performed but the building of theatre spaces specifically to support it did cease. Instead, theatre spaces became more *environmental,* meaning that performances took place in spaces that already existed, sometimes in people's houses, in marketplaces, and in churches. It is this latter location that we must look at in some depth as history moves out of the Dark Ages and into the medieval era or Middle Ages (800–1400 AD).

The Medieval Era

One of the most defining developments of the Western World after the Fall of Rome was the rise of Christianity. For years an illegal religion, the Christian faith was able to quite literally come out of the basement with the Fall of Rome. As churches were built and congregations grew throughout the Dark and Middle Ages, the churches realized they had significant challenges ahead of them.

Hundreds of years of relative social disarray meant that there had been fewer academic opportunities for the people in general and many of the laity were now illiterate meaning they could not read the Bible. Additionally, Bibles were generally not printed in the common language of the people but instead were written in Latin. Similarly, church services were often performed in Latin meaning that churchgoers also couldn't understand what was being said to them. So the Church had a significant dilemma on their hands—how do we teach our members the stories of the Bible? How do we teach them how to avoid Hell and get into Heaven? How do we do all of this when they can neither read the Bible nor understand the services? They turned to theatre for the answers.

Initially, *liturgical drama* was primarily comprised of a selection of scenes from the Bible or lives of the saints, chosen by the clergy and reenacted for their members right inside the church. They used *mansions* which were set pieces designed to look like the significant locations needed for the particular scene chosen. These mansions were arranged in the church in such a way that a series of scenes could be performed.

Two of the most common set pieces used were the Heaven and Hell mansions which were located at opposite ends of the stage and were quite convincingly decorated. It was the intent to make Heaven look as desirable a location as possible and was quite beautiful while the Hell mansion was quite the opposite. Ultimately the message they wanted to convey was that you want to go to Heaven and avoid Hell at all costs. Many of these performances were tied to significant times of the year with Easter being one of the most common.

Eventually these series, or *cycles*, of plays became so large and time- and space-consuming that they could no longer be performed inside the church. They were moved outside onto raised stages. With the move outside came opportunities for the mansions to become larger and even more elaborate. These theatre spaces were now referred to as **Hell Mouth stages** because they were now typically dominated by a large set piece representing Hell that often resembled a large fire-breathing monster.

The audiences enjoyed special effects with their entertainment and it was common to see a Hell Mouth breathing smoke and flames while screaming sinners were pulled into it or horned and tailed devils came out if it. On the opposite end of the stage was Heaven and again, all the stops were pulled out to ensure a clear message—this was a place you desired to be. The temple-like structure of the Heaven mansion was often covered in silver leaf and lit with candles to make it glow from inside. Again, the message was clear—this was a desirable place to be.

Another challenge that the Church faced was in reaching the people in the smaller villages outside of the cities. It was hard for the smaller churches to afford such elaborate performances, so instead the performances were brought to them. **Wagon stages** or *pageant wagons* were created to serve as moveable mansions.

The set locations were built atop a wheeled cart, much like a modern parade float, and were then accompanied by musicians and other performers as they travelled from one village to another. Many of the little villages had raised platforms the wagons could pull up to thus extending their playable stage space. The villagers could then gather around the wagons and view each individual scene.

Not all of the theatre that was being performed during the Middle Ages was religious in nature. Other types of entertainment were regularly offered via *wagon stages,* in banqueting halls and in marketplaces. But you'll notice that all of these locations have something in common: none of them was a permanent location built specifically for the purpose of performing theatre. After the Fall of Rome, it is not until the relative stability and prosperity of the Renaissance that we next see buildings being constructed solely for the presentation of theatrical entertainment.

The Renaissance

Renaissance literally means "rebirth." This time period began in Italy as early as the fourteenth century and lasted through the middle of the seventeenth century as ideas slowly spread throughout Europe. It was during this time period that many additional advances were made in the development of theatre spaces and the design of theatrical scenery.

With advancements in engineering and technology, one of the most significant changes to the theatre spaces was the move indoors. Now with the ability to light indoor spaces through the use of candles and oil lamps, theatre artists were free to move indoors to perform their plays. This change also meant that artists were now free to explore new possibilities with scenery because weather was no longer a concern for them.

Considered to be one of the earliest indoor theatres ever built and known as the oldest surviving Renaissance theatre, the Teatro Olimpico was built between 1580 and 1584 in Vicenza, Italy.

There was a renewed interest during this time period in the theatre of the ancient Greeks and Romans. The architect Andrea Palladio attempted to recreate indoors what he believed an outdoor Roman theatre looked like. Even the stage wall resembles a Roman *scaenae frons.* What is new here, though, is what appears in the openings in that stage wall.

A view of the stage and scenic background of *Teatro Olimpico.*

One of the most significant innovations of the Renaissance was Filippo Brunelleschi's work with *perspective drawing.* This concept, which allows artists to convincingly portray distance in their work, was another instrumental development that led to the popularity of theatrical scenery. So popular was this concept, that artists even took it a step further to create *forced perspective* which allows an artist to portray even more depth in a three-dimensional work than would be there naturally. What this meant at the Teatro Olimpico was that Palladio was able to add alleys referred to as 'vistas' behind the stage wall which gave the impression of long streets lined with buildings. In fact, these alleys were quite short but the use of *forced perspective* gave the audience the illusion that entire city

A detailed view through one of the vistas on the stage of *Teatro Olimpico.*

A view of the stage and the seating area of *Teatro Olimpico.*

blocks extended into the distance. Also, the views were located in such a way that all of the audience members would be able to see down at least one of them, giving them all the same relative experience. There were disadvantages to this type of scenery however. Actors were not able to perform within the views because, only a few feet down the alley, the difference in scales would cause the actor to actually appear larger than the buildings they were standing next to. Obviously this would ruin the intended effect of the scenery. While an interesting novelty, this specific use of perspective scenery did not become widely popular.

Another artist who exploited the development of perspective drawing for use in a theatrical setting was Sebastiano Serlio (1475-1554 AD). Serlio is known for creating a type of scenery that suited all styles of plays and was transportable. Initially, he created a set of three painted backdrops, one comic, one tragic, and one pastoral (set in an outdoor location).

These backdrops could be rolled up and moved to wherever a performance might be taking place. His perspective paintings on canvas gave the audience the illusion of depth and space where there wasn't any and helped them to understand the physical location of the play.

Eventually these flat painted backdrops were made partially three-dimensional. Using techniques similar to those used by Palladio at the Teatro Olimpico, Serlio and other theatre designers began to explore how to improve upon the illusion of space in the scenery they created for theatres. Eventually the actors were able to inhabit part of the three dimensional set, further adding to the illusion created for the audience.

Another historically important building constructed during the Renaissance was the Teatro Farnese. This theatre, still standing in Parma, Italy, was completed in 1618 and is recognized as one of the earliest examples of a proscenium style theatre. The audience's desire for realistic scenery had grown after the initial developments introduced by Serlio and other theatre artists and it was only a matter of time before architects realized the advantages of presenting perspective scenery behind a proscenium frame. As the need to change scenery during the performances increased, further developments were made in an effort to make the changes happen more effectively.

One of the most significant developments, which is still in use today especially in opera and ballet, was the **wing and drop system**. This system took the ideas Serlio had developed and made them even more three-dimensional by placing some of the painted scenery on the wings that flanked the sides of the stage, and the rest on a painted backdrop which hung at the back. This opened a large playing space for the actors while still giving the illusion that they were surrounded by three-dimensional scenery.

One of the next steps in the development of realistic three-dimensional scenery was created by a designer named Giacomo Torelli. He created a new method called the **chariot and pole system**. This system consisted of drops and painted scenery wings attached through the stage floor to a wheeled wagon below the stage. The chariot and poles were then attached to a pulley system that a lone stagehand could turn. Since these mechanisms were unseen by the audience, the scenery appeared to change as if by magic. This revolutionized the possibilities of scene design and Torelli exploited this to full advantage with fantastic and beautiful designs like no one had ever seen before.

Such was the desire for elaborate scenery that playwrights began to write plays specifically designed to require the elaborate effects audiences were becoming accustomed to. In fact, sketches of some performances of the seventeenth and eighteenth centuries illustrate vividly how focus had begun to shift from well-thought-out plots and characters to extensive and impressive scenic changes. In some cases the scenery even upstaged the actors completely.

Another type of theatre that became very influential in Europe during the Renaissance were the Spanish **corrales** or courtyard theatres.

Buildings in Spain and other areas of Europe in this era typically made use of a central courtyard which gave the advantage of being able to allow more light into

A scenic background designed by Sebastiano Serlio for a tragic play.

The wooden Teatro Farnese built in 1618 in Parma, Italy.

© Sergio Pitamitz/Corbis

The proscenium and stage of the Teatro Farnese built in 1618 in Parma, Italy.

the rooms. This presented a very natural location for a theatre performance to occur as they not only had space to set up a raised platform at one end of the courtyard, they also had space for audience on the ground level and on the balconies above. This type of theatre was so popular, in fact, that it proved to be the inspiration for one of the single most famous theatre buildings ever built, Shakespeare's Globe Theatre.

The Globe Theatre was one of a group of playhouses known as Elizabethan public theatres. Owing a debt to the Spanish *corrales* that preceded them, the Elizabethan theatres were all built in London, England and were quite striking in appearance. Most were constructed as freestanding multisided buildings that appeared round from a distance.

The stage of an Elizabethan playhouse is dominated by the main structure known as the *tiring house* which provided not only a place for actors to enter and exit from and to put on costumes, but also provided storage as well as a roofed area housing machinery that was used to lower scenery and actors into place when needed. The flag that flew from the roof of the tiring house announced for quite some distance what style of play would be performed at that theatre that day. The Globe Theatre is also known as Shakespeare's Theatre because it is the building in which many of his plays were presented for the first time.

© Dorling Kindersley/Getty Images.

Illustration of a typical Elizabethan style theatre.

After civil war broke out in England in 1642, the theatres were closed and it wasn't until 1660 that theatre began to be actively presented again. By then, most of the Elizabethan theatres had been demolished or had fallen into disrepair. Additionally, the ideas and style of theatre being developed in Italy during the Renaissance had begun to make their way north. When theatres began to be built again in England in the later seventeenth century, they followed the Italianate rather than the Elizabethan style.

Once audiences and theatre artists had gotten a taste of the possibilities available with proscenium style houses and wing-and-drop perspective scenery, this style continued to develop over the next two centuries. The proscenium theatres of the seventeenth and eighteenth centuries began to make use of the **pit, box, and gallery** seating style which allowed audience members to sit on benches on the floor (the pit), private or semi private rooms on the second and third levels (boxes), or in seats above the boxes, high above the stage floor (the gallery).

Some of these proscenium theatres were quite ornate like Margrave's Opera House in Germany, while others such as the Chestnut Street Theatre in Philadelphia were rather plain. In any case, the proscenium-style theatre had developed a following and a tradition that has continued into the modern day. If asked to describe the layout of a typical theatre space, many audience members today would describe a proscenium theatre. This is interesting given that with 2,500 years of theatre history behind us, the proscenium theatre is relatively new.

Conclusion

Theatre spaces have changed over time, and our contemporary theatre contains many historical features. By examining the evolution of theatrical space we can identify the shifting relationships between audiences, technological advancements, acting styles, and dramatic literature. Furthermore, we are able to understand the role that theatre has played in the shaping of our civilization. Given this rich history, contemporary practitioners can make decisions about theatrical space and audience configuration to impact the audience experience.

THEATRE ORGANIZATIONS

Colleen Reilly

CHAPTER OBJECTIVES

- Distinguish between producing and presenting organizations.
- Identify the primary differences between commercial and nonprofit theatre organizations.
- Discuss the characteristics of Regional, Educational, and Community Theatre nonprofit theatres.
- Define Broadway and Off-Broadway theatre organizations.
- Identify the major labor unions that support professional theatre.

I n this chapter the term "theatre" refers not only to the artistic activity, but also includes the organization that presents the artistic activity, and the physical building. That is, a theatre can make theatre in a theatre. Theatres exist across the United States in major urban destinations, regional centers, and local communities. Theatre in these places can be created by practitioners who are professionals, earning their livelihood from the theatrical projects. It can also be created by nonprofessional practitioners who participate in theatre projects, but do not support themselves solely through theatrical endeavors. Since theatre is a collaborative process, theatre organizations are formed to promote and sustain theatrical activity.

AMATEUR VERSUS PROFESSIONAL

For the purposes of this text, the distinction between amateur and professional practitioners is solely a matter of compensation. Professional practitioners subsist on the income generated from their participation in the theatre as artists, administrators, educators, or consultants. In some cases the term "professional" is used if the practitioner receives any compensation, even if that income does not support them completely; for our purposes we will refer to this as "semi-professional." Amateur practitioners operate on a volunteer basis. These categories do not necessarily address the quality of theatre created and presented.

Because theatre cannot exist without the simultaneous presence of a theatre space, a practitioner, a dramatic action, and an audience, there are many costs associated with producing theatre. Physical theatres must be maintained or rented. Professional practitioners must be compensated. Plays are intellectual property and must be licensed. Audiences must be reached through marketing.

Consider then the limitations of theatre revenue. Other businesses might increase the availability of the product to drive up income, but theatres are limited by fixed capacities and labor restrictions. The materials required to stage the action of a production can be expensive, and are often consumed in the course of a single production. Audiences resist exorbitant prices and most often purchase tickets to a theatre production as a one-time venture.

There are two primary business models for theatrical organizations: nonprofit and commercial. **Nonprofit theatre** is driven by an artistic vision, and sees theatre as a public service. Commercial theatre is driven by a profit motive and views theatre as a commodity of goods and services that can be exchanged with consumers. Simply put, nonprofit theatre pursues the creation of theatrical art as its main objective. Commercial theatre is driven by the potential to make money. This chapter will examine different types of theatrical organizations and the ways in which they contribute to the process of creating theatre.

Whether commercial or nonprofit, theatre organizations can also be distinguished as producing or presenting organizations. A *producing organization* creates the theatrical project and is responsible for all of the steps in the rehearsal and production process: selecting the project, casting, rehearsing, and performing. Producing organizations sometimes own or have access to their own theatre spaces, but may also rent or secure a theatre for the run of the show. *Presenting organizations* do not create the theatrical project but "book" the production to appear for their audiences. Presenting organizations often manage their own theatrical spaces, or are associated with performing arts festivals which allow for multiple booking.

At Slippery Rock University the Department of Theatre could be considered a *producing organization*. The department models the standards of a professional theatre organization in its season selection, auditions, rehearsals, and productions. Alternatively, the Kaleidoscope Arts Festival would be considered a *presenting organization* that brings performing arts events to campus by booking outside artists and supporting campus appearance by performing artists on tour. Likewise, Slippery Rock University is the *presenting organization* for the Performing Arts Series. Each of these organizations utilizes the same spaces on campus.

Nonprofit Theatres

Nonprofit theatres are organizations with special tax-exempt status. Nonprofit theatre organizations are guided by their *mission statements*. These describe the purpose, value, and activities of the organization.

Consider the mission statement of Pittsburgh's Quantum Theatre:

QUANTUM THEATRE is a kind of laboratory, an incubator for the amazing, christened in 1990, rededicated each year with the rites of spring to its mission to bring forth artists forging new theatrical ground.

They are playwrights, directors, actors, influencers. They come from Pittsburgh, from around the country, and from around the world. Productions are staged environmentally in places that aren't theatres. Quantum's artists mine all kinds of non-traditional spaces for the sensory possibilities they offer when combined with creative design. We find it meaningful to place the audience and performers together, the moving parts inside the works.

The shows run the gamut from those you thought you knew but now experience like never before, to shows that didn't exist until their elements mixed in our laboratory. Sometimes there's singing. Often a sunset. Always a reaction.

We want to move people with our experiments. We believe that the theatre has limitless ability to put people in motion. If any art can transform, open a mind, the theatre can. We are interested in real life and how it intersects with a theatrical experience—resulting in plays staged outside where a moon may rise, or not, or an urban excavation where street noises will infiltrate, or a warehouse in winter where the audience might need blankets... then watch a performer strip naked and take a shower. We're looking for truthfulness, knowing that the word is a slippery slope. We give voice to artists who invest deeply and touch the personal, even as they tell a tale, a far-off, magical, scary, too-close-to-home, knee-slapping, sob-inducing tale. (http://www.quantumtheatre.com/)

Reprinted by permission of Quantum Theater.

The purpose of a nonprofit organization must be charitable, cultural, or educational in nature. Nonprofit theatres, therefore, have mission statements that often include statements about the services that they provide to their communities.

There is a common misconception that the term "nonprofit" means that these kinds of organizations do not make any money. However, "nonprofit" or "not-for-profit" actually refers to a special tax-exempt status afforded to organizations that meet federal criteria for public service. This status is the 501(c)3 and in order to qualify for it organizations must go through a rigorous federal application process. Nonprofit organizations generate significant revenue, but in order to maintain nonprofit status any surplus must be applied towards supporting the organization's mission and not towards the compensation of individual staff or management.

There are many kinds of organizations that fall under the description of nonprofit theatres. These include regional theatres, educational theatres, and community theatres. Each one was developed to meet a specific need for its audience. *Regional theatres* create opportunities to attend professional theatre outside of major urban areas like New York City. *Educational theatres* promote participation in theatre experiences by offering performances and instruction, and are often staffed by professional theatre artists. *Community theatres* provide nonprofessionals the prospect to create theatre, and promote theatre appreciation.

REGIONAL THEATRE
Professional nonprofit theatre organizations, also called resident theatres.
EDUCATIONAL THEATRE
Professional or semi-professional nonprofit theatre companies whose primary goal is to provide theatre opportunities and education to primary, secondary, and post-secondary schools.
COMMUNITY THEATRE
Amateur or volunteer theatre organizations in residence in specific neighborhoods or regions.

Regional theatres are also often referred to as *resident theatres*. Regional theatres operate under annual *seasons*, or series of productions. Choosing these seasons is determined by a variety of factors including the availability of company artists, the need for generating ticket revenue, and the organization's mission statement. Sometimes a regional theatre is also a repertory company. A *repertory theatre* is a company comprised of the same professional artists who stage multiple plays in a given season.

Regional theatres are highly visible and lasting members of an area's cultural landscape. For example, the Pittsburgh Public Theater was established in 1974 on the city's North Side. It moved downtown to the O'Reilly Theater in 1999, and opened the new space with a production of Pittsburgh native playwright August Wilson's *King Hedley II*. The mission statement of this resident theatre is as follows:

The mission of Pittsburgh Public Theater is to provide artistically diverse theatrical experiences of the highest quality. Pittsburgh Public Theater also strives to serve, challenge, stimulate and entertain while operating in a fiscally responsible manner. The Public shares its resources with the community through education and outreach initiatives intended for a wide range of people with the goal of expanding and diversifying the audience while enriching the community.

Reprinted by permission of Pittsburgh Public Theater.

Educational theatre nonprofits provide theatre instruction and present theatre for schools at the primary, secondary, undergraduate, and graduate levels. They can be training grounds for emerging theatre professionals, or create more casual encounters with theatre in matinee presentations, school tours, and extracurricular courses. Most nonprofit theatre organizations have a department dedicated to outreach and education to fulfill the requirement of a nonprofit mission that provides a public service. However, educational theatres are entirely devoted to instruction about theatre or through theatre.

CREATIVE DRAMA

In the 1920s theatre practitioner Winifred Ward created a method of using theatre activities to promote learning across the elementary school curriculum. Ward developed exercises based on pantomime, dialogue, and characterization that she called "creative drama." In 1944 she launched the National Children's Theatre Conference which exists today as the American Alliance for Theatre and Education (AATE).

Community theatre nonprofits generally exist as amateur organizations. The participants in community theatres generally support themselves through otherprofessional means, and do not rely on theatrical activity to provide their income. Community theatres often operate on a volunteer basis, and are focused on providing theatre events in areas that are underserved by commercial, regional, or educational theatres.

Nonprofit theatre organizations are vital to the livelihood of theatre as an art form, and they contribute to the professionalization of theatre arts. Since 1990, the number of nonprofit theatres in the United States has doubled. These theatres are staffed by professionals in **arts administration**. Arts administration or arts management positions support the activities of the organization and align those activities with the organizational mission. Under the supervision of the nonprofit *board of directors*, or governing body, arts administrators execute the marketing, budgets, fund-raising, and programming of nonprofit organizations.

Nonprofit theatre organizations tend to divide their management functions into two positions: the *artistic director* and the *managing director*. The artistic director considers the mission of the nonprofit organization and creates the program of activities and productions to reflect it. The artistic director selects and supervises the practitioners employed or involved with the nonprofit organization: the directors, actors, and designers. The *managing director* oversees the buildings and facilities for the organization, as well as providing supervision for the administrative staff.

Commercial Organizations

Commercial organizations rely on profits from receipts and earned income. Commercial organizations are not guided by mission statements; instead they operate under the profit motive. While commercial organizations have an interest in creating artistically challenging productions, they do so with an eye to projected ticket sales, corporate sponsorship, and potential merchandising. If their proposed production does not have a "hook" for the public, it will not succeed.

When a theatrical production is mounted in a commercial environment, it is referred to as a *property*. A **theatrical property** contains the financial interests of all of the contributors to the production, and provides a model by which everyone who contributes to the production can be compensated systematically. The theatrical *producer* manages the property, including raising the funds to create the production, promoting the production, and overseeing all of the staff and administrative functions of the production.

One of the major differences between nonprofit and commercial theatres is the life cycle of the organization. Nonprofit theatre organizations apply for a permanent status of incorporation, and only dissolve as a corporate entity under extreme circumstances. Commercial producers incorporate as an LLC (limited liability corporation) and dissolve as soon as the ability of a single production to make a profit declines. Furthermore, nonprofit theatre organizations are public corporations and must openly declare their financial statements. Commercial theatre organizations are often privatized, and their financial records are not a matter of public record.

Commercial organizations have to produce theatre in an environment that has a proven market for theatre, and appropriate venues. For this reason, New York City's Broadway district has emerged as the most significant location for commercial producing. The term "Broadway" has become synonymous with "commercial theatre," but there are some nonprofit organizations that produce there. A Broadway production is any performance that plays in a professional venue in New York City that has over 499 seats. Most of these venues, or theatres, are located in a geographical area in Manhattan referred to as the "Broadway Box." There are 40 **Broadway theatres**.

Broadway Theatres

Ambassador	**Cort**	**Longacre**	**Palace**
219 W. 49th Street	138 W. 48th Street	220 W. 48th Street	1564 Broadway
1,088 seats	1,082 seats	1,091 seats	1,740 seats
Shubert Organization	Shubert Organization	Shubert Organization	Nederlander Organization
American Airlines	**Foxwoods Theatre**	**Lunt-Fontanne**	**Richard Rodgers**
227 W. 42nd Street	213 W. 42nd Street	205 W. 46th Street	226 W. 46th St.
740 seats	1,319 seats	1,505 seats	1,319 seats
Roundabout Theatre Co.	Live Nation	Nederlander Organization	Nederlander Organization
Brooks Atkinson	**Samuel J. Friedman**	**Lyceum**	**St. James**
256 W. 47th Street	261 West 47th St.	149 W. 45th Street	246 W. 44th Street
1,069 seats	650 seats	922 seats	1,644 seats
Nederlander Organization	Manhattan Theatre Club	Shubert Organization	Jujamcyn Theatres
Ethel Barrymore	**Gershwin**	**Majestic**	**Gerald Schoenfeld**
243 W. 47th Street	222 W. 51st Street	245 W. 44th Street	236 W. 45th Street
1,058 seats	1,900 seats	1,645 seats	1,079 seats
Shubert Organization	Nederlander Organization	Shubert Organization	Shubert Organization
Vivian Beaumont	**John Golden**	**Marquis**	**Shubert**
150 W. 65th Street	252 W. 45th Street	1535 Broadway	225 W. 44th Street
1,080 seats	804 seats	1,611 seats	1,460 seats
Lincoln Center	Shubert Organization	Nederlander Organization	Shubert Organization
Belasco	**Helen Hayes**	**Minskoff**	**Neil Simon**
111 W. 44th Street	240 W. 44th Street	200 W. 45th Street	250 W. 52nd Street
1,016 seats	597 seats	1,597 seats	1,445 seats
Shubert Organization	Independent	Nederlander Organization	Nederlander Organization
Booth	**Al Hirschfeld**	**Music Box**	**Stephen Sondheim**
222 W. 45th Street	302 W. 45th Street	239 W. 45th Street	124 West 43rd Street
766 seats	1,292 seats	1,009 seats	1,055 seats
Shubert Organization	Jujamcyn Theatres	Shubert Organization	Roundabout Theatre Co.

Continued			
Broadhurst	**Imperial**	**Nederlander**	**Studio 54**
235 W. 44th Street	249 W. 45th Street	208 W. 41st Street	254 W. 54th Street
1,156 seats	1,443 seats	1,232 seats	1,015 seats
Shubert Organization	Shubert Organization	Nederlander Organization	Roundabout Theatre Co.
Broadway	**Bernard B. Jacobs**	**New Amsterdam**	**August Wilson**
1681 Broadway	242 W. 45th Street	214 W. 42nd Street	245 W. 52nd Street
1,761 seats	1,078 seats	1,800 seats	1,222 seats
Shubert Organization	Shubert Organization	Disney	Jujamcyn Theatres
Circle in the Square	**Walter Kerr**	**Eugene O'Neill**	**Winter Garden**
1633 Broadway	219 W. 48th Street	230 W. 49th Street	1634 Broadway
623 seats	949 seats	1,065 seats	1,526 seats
Independent	Jujamcyn Theatres	Jujamcyn Theatres	Shubert Organization

BROADWAY
Any professional or nonprofit theatre production that plays in a venue that has over 499 seats and is located in the area known as the "Broadway Box."

A Broadway production has several unique characteristics, the most significant of which is the cost. In order to mount a Broadway play a producer must raise an estimated $2 million to front the expenses incurred from the conception of the project to the opening night. Broadway musicals can require a minimum of $11 million. This does not include the weekly production costs during the run of a show which include artistic and technical staff, space and equipment rental, and union fees and dues. Producing theatre on Broadway is a high risk venture that will be discussed further in Chapter 8.

Off-Broadway productions are another example of largely commercial theatre. An Off-Broadway production is any professional commercial or nonprofit production that plays in a New York City venue of 99–499 seats. Off-Broadway productions allow commercial organizations to stage productions that are appropriate for smaller audiences at lower costs. It requires an estimated $800,000 to produce a play Off-Broadway and a meager $1.2 million to stage a musical.

Not all commercial theatre is contained in New York City, but the vast majority of for-profit enterprises are staged there. Substantial commercial theatre can also be found in Las Vegas. Outside of the United States, commercial theatre thrives in London's West End, a district similar to Broadway in the designation of theatre size and the kinds of productions staged. However, the majority of theatre produced across the United States is non-profit.

Given the primary objective of generating revenue, many commercial productions tour in addition to their run in commercial theatre districts. Touring productions allow commercial theatre organizations to maximize ticket revenue and merchandising while raising the profile of a particular production.

Wicked, a musical with music and lyrics by Stephen Schwartz and book by Winnie Holzman, is based on a 1995 novel by Gregory Maguire which is a revision of the 1900 children's story by L. Frank Baum adapted for the 1939 film, *The Wizard of Oz*. *Wicked* opened on Broadway at the Gershwin Theatre in 2003. The commercial producers included Universal Pictures, The Araca Group, John B. Platt, Marc Platt, and David Stone. *Wicked* has broken international box-office records and has played on Broadway and London's West End. The production has undertaken its second North American tour in addition to being licensed for productions in Germany, Japan, and Australia.

Theatre Unions

Commercial theatre organizations are fully unionized, and many professional nonprofit theatre organizations participate in unions or uphold union standards for contract negotiations, working conditions, and salary and wage scales. There are three main unions that act on behalf of professional theatre practitioners: the Actors' Equity Association (AEA), the Stage Directors and Choreographers Society (SDC) and the International Alliance of Theatrical Stage Employees (IATSE).

Playwrights are not associated with a union; however, they are supported by a professional organization known as The Dramatists Guild. The Dramatists Guild serves playwrights, lyricists, and composers and makes recommendations on compensation, royalties, and intellectual property. These recommendations include the right to be present throughout the casting, rehearsal, and production process.

The Actors' Equity Association (AEA) was founded in 1913 and currently represents more than 48,000 professional actors and stage managers. The Actors' Equity Association protects its members with minimum salary standards, guidelines for compensation, safety issues, insured wages, health benefits, pensions, and access to audition notices. Actors and stage managers must earn entry into the Actors' Equity Association by being hired under an Equity contract, being a member of a sister union, or completing the Equity Membership Candidate program. Once accepted into the Actors' Equity Association, members must remain current on their payment of dues and meet professional standards of conduct.

The Stage Directors and Choreographers Society (SDC) was created in 1959 and shares similar primary responsibilities with the Actors' Equity Association of contract negotiations, health benefits, pensions, and industry announcements. The Stage Directors and Choreographers Society also frequently addresses issues of intellectual property in terms of the vision of stage directors and choreographers. This protects the integrity of production concepts and choices made by professional directors and choreographers in response to particular productions, and allows directors and choreographers to protect their artistic work.

The International Alliance of Theatrical Stage Employees (IATSE) was established in 1893 and protects professionals in all theatre crafts including scenic artists, stagehands, costumers, and front-of-house workers. The union was founded largely to create collective bargaining around safety standards, but over time has broadened its focus to compensation and professionalization. The International Alliance of Theatrical Stage Employees is the largest of all professional theatre unions, and most physical theatres require members of IATSE on staff.

In addition to unions for theatre practitioners, there are collective bargaining units that negotiate contracts on behalf of producing organizations. These include the Broadway League, the League of Off-Broadway Theatres and Producers, and the League of Resident Theatres (LORT). The League of Resident Theatres negotiates on behalf of nonprofit regional theatres, and has seventy-four member theatres in twenty-nine states, including six member theatres in Pennsylvania.

Conclusion

Theatre organizations exist to support theatrical endeavors in the commercial and nonprofit sectors. There are two types of theatre organizations: producing theatres and presenting organizations. Nonprofit theatres are guided by their public service mission statements and can be either professional regional theatres, semi-professional educational theatres, or amateur community theatres. Commercial theatre organizations are driven by a profit motive and must negotiate contracts with practitioners through theatre unions.

MAKING THEATRE

Colleen Reilly

Theatre is a highly collaborative art form. The major contributors to a theatrical performance include the Director, Actors, Playwright, Producer, and Designers. Each of these roles requires creativity, persistence, and expertise.

Consider the title "practitioner." It suggests the idea of "practice." In order to be successful in the theatre you must accumulate experience in the practice of your craft. Practitioners may have very different skill sets; however, they have the need to practice their skills very much in common.

In this section we will take a closer look at theatre practitioners. Who are they? What do they do? How do they contribute to making meaning in the theatre? We will also examine how practitioners collaborate in the rehearsal process.

DIRECTORS

David Skeele and Laura Smiley

CHAPTER OBJECTIVES

- Identify the history of the modern director.
- Define "concept."
- Describe the process of casting including typecasting and nontraditional casting.
- Consider the role of the director in the making of meaning in the theatre.
- Recognize different directing approaches.

O ften, when studying the role of the director, an Introduction to Theatre student will ask, "Has there always been a director?" It's a seemingly simple question, one with an interesting answer. The modern notion of the director as a single, stand-alone theatre artist who interprets the play, coaches the actors and coordinates every design element, has been with us for fewer than 150 years (a mere heartbeat in the roughly 2,500-year history of organized theatre). However, that is not to suggest that until the late nineteenth century theatrical productions were formless free-for-alls. There has always been someone or some*thing* (I'll explain that one in a moment) guiding theatre artists as they prepare plays for performance.

In the theatre of the ancient Greeks, the playwright (who was called **didaskalos**— "the teacher") took it upon himself to convey the meaning of the play to his actors, to choreograph the movement and, presumably, to supervise the construction of masks and costumes. The medieval "pageant master" was, like the modern director, a stand-alone artist who coached his amateur actors and coordinated what were sometimes complex technical effects. The leading actors of eighteenth- and nineteenth-century productions (called "actor-managers)" were the unquestioned "bosses" of the performance process. Why then do we say that that directing is a "new" or "modern" theatre element?

> **DIDASKALOS**
> From the ancient Greek, meaning "teacher," the playwright who instructed the performers in meaning and movement and who presumably oversaw the making of masks and costumes.

The answer is that theatre in the "modern" era (coinciding with the an era usually defined as beginning in the Industrial Age in the mid-nineteenth century) is starkly different from the theatre of previous eras. In the theatre of ancient Greece or medieval France or eighteenth-century England there existed very few *options* about how theatre should be produced. In eighteenth-century England, for instance, every audience member entered the theatre knowing they would see the cast assembled into a "horseshoe" configuration on the stage, with the lead

KEY TERMS

Antiquarianism
Casting
Conventions
Didaskalos
Realism
Spine
Typecasting

actor standing center stage (where the best light was) and the other cast members ringed around him. "Staging" consisted mostly of stepping into and out of the light cast by the central chandelier. They would expect to see actors clad in the fashions of their own time, with little or no effort spent on evoking the specifics of a different time period. Certainly there would be little question of interpretation of the pieces being presented. The actor-manager would make sure that everyone was making sense of the speeches, but there would be an assumption that the play had a single meaning that would be shared by every audience member.

These expectations—really unspoken agreements between the audience and the theatre artists—are called **conventions**, and in earlier times conventions tended to be so specific that they left little room for directorial choices. It could be said that in theatrical eras controlled by strict conventions the *culture*, more than any single person, existed as the director.

A *convention* is essentially an unspoken agreement between the performers and the audience. For instance, when a performer steps away from the performer with whom she is speaking, leans toward the audience and speaks a line in a *stage whisper*, the audience accepts that it is supposed to believe the other character cannot hear what is being said. This is a convention called an *aside*, and the audience usually agrees to accept it in an otherwise realistic play, even though it is patently unrealistic. Similarly, the audience accepts the convention of *holding for laughs*—the performers pausing while audience laughter dies down enough for their next lines to be heard—even though such pauses would not normally be taken in a real conversation.

—David Skeele

Forerunners of Modern Directors

Caroline Neuber was one of Europe's first female actor-managers. She created a theatre with her husband, actor Johann Neuber, and joined forces with Johann Gottsched who was a leading intellectual in Germany in the mid-eighteenth century. Her idea was to reform the theatre by raising production standards and improving artistic product. In imitation of French neoclassical writers she replaced older plays full of comedic stock characters with more serious dramatic efforts. Instead of improvisation she instituted carefully rehearsed scenes. Actors were given duties like painting the set or sewing costumes in addition to playing their roles. By the end of her lifetime, this new theatre technique was copied by other companies throughout Germany.

In an effort to overcome the bad reputations that actors had, Neuber monitored their personal lives (can you imagine?)

—Laura Smiley

In England at around the same time, David Garrick is often thought of as the forerunner of the modern director. As a partner in the Drury Lane Theatre in London, Garrick, who was also the company's leading performer, was responsible for all major artistic choices. He believed in a more natural approach to acting and was quite a disciplinarian as well. He required his actors to be on time, lines memorized and "acted" not simply recited. His rehearsal periods sometimes stretched into weeks as he pushed his actors to develop their characters fully with research and preparation.

In the nineteenth century, many forces converged which challenged and broadened theatrical conventions. One was a renewed interest in history that had begun a century earlier (fueled largely by the excavations of well-preserved historical sites such as Pompeii and Herculaneum). As knowledge grew about the architecture and clothing of ancient times, so did interest in bringing historically accurate detail onto the stage. By the mid-nineteenth century, actor-managers such as Charles Kean and William Charles Macready were not only concerned keeping lesser actors out of their light, but with making sure that costume crews and scene painters were getting their historical facts right.

This trend in theatrical production was called *antiquarianism*, and among some directors of classical texts it continues to exist today. **Antiquarianism** is a movement in the production of classic plays (usually associated with the works of Shakespeare), that attempts to create authentic historical details.

—David Skeele

Creating perfectly accurate history on stage ended up being such a painstaking, time-consuming affair that it became difficult for an actor (especially one playing enormous leading roles) to manage it, and it is no accident that some of the finest antiquarian productions of the age were staged by a man who had little interest in performing himself. Georg II, the Duke of Saxe-Meiningen, considered by many to be the father of modern directing, was one of the first to take an objective step back from the performance process and concentrate solely on supervision of the production. Under his tutelage the Meiningen Players, as his company was called, were able to not only offer dazzling productions of classic plays, but also put together some of the most comprehensive historical costume and properties collections the world had ever seen.

However, it was not only the immaculate antiquarianism of the Meiningen Players' productions that distinguished them. The Duke's work also intersected with another, more significant movement that was raging throughout Europe: the movement known as **realism**. It was not merely history that people wished to see reflected more accurately, but reality.

We run the risk of getting sidetracked here (and of duplicating material covered in other chapters), but in brief, realism sprang from the sense that theatre ought to more accurately reflect the conditions in which people lived. The Industrial Age saw a major economic shift from agriculture to manufacture and a rapid expansion of urban areas, and along with that shift and expansion came grinding poverty and subhuman working conditions. As pervasive as these horrible conditions were, for a long time one could find no trace of them on the stage—instead, audiences found only the usual romantic tales of heroes and kings. Some playwrights revolted and began writing plays that explored the social issues of the day, ones that took place in everyday drawing rooms and workplaces.

REALISM

In the late nineteenth century, plays began to depict characters and situations close to everyday life. Three playwrights perfected this style: Anton Chekhov of Russia, Henrik Ibsen of Norway, and August Strindberg of Sweden. It was called realism because the plays resembled situations that people could identify with and verify from their own personal experiences. This placed great demands on the actors who had to play as realistically as possible with no trace of superficiality or fakery. Konstantin Stanislavski created an acting system to attain this level of believability in acting.

It deserves mention that Henrik Ibsen and August Strindberg did not confine themselves to writing realistic plays. Ibsen's later plays are linked to a movement called *symbolism*, a style that stressed the symbolic essence of things over the photographic representation of reality, and most of Strindberg's work is classified as *expressionism* (see below). However, much of Ibsen's "middle period" work, especially plays such as *Ghosts, Hedda Gabler* and *A Doll House*, were considered at the time to be spectacularly shocking and vulgar examples of realism, and at least a couple of Strindberg's plays—*The Father* and *Miss Julie*—scandalized audiences with their frank, realistic depictions of the battle of the sexes.

—David Skeele

Even in productions of less-realistic plays (such as those of Shakespeare), audiences were now demanding more life-like effects. Many actor-managers, caught up in their own performances and slow to react to changing conventions, continued to stage in the old manner, for instance offering *crowd scenes* that consisted of lines of extras wearing third-generation hand-me-down costumes gaping stupidly at the audience. The Duke of Saxe-Meiningen, however, was appalled by this, and introduced innovations such as making sure every character, no matter how minor, was clothed in period costume, and that every "crowd" was actually several groups, each under the supervision of an experienced actor. The effect was breathtakingly new and different for audiences, and his productions helped stoke the new hunger for realistic illusion.

It helped that he was a Duke, and could afford it.   — Laura Smiley

The new realistic work by dramatists such as Thomas Robertson in England and Henrik Ibsen in Norway represented an even bigger challenge to the old ways. Orchestrating a realistic scene in, say, a crowded family home, where audience focus had to shift between different groups of characters, was nearly impossible for someone who was simultaneously acting in a lead role.

Realism was not the only movement fueling the rise of the modern director. The late nineteenth century and early twentieth century saw an explosion of dramatic movements that reacted against the limits of realism. There was, for instance, *expressionism*, which attempted to capture the turbulent inner state of dream and nightmare and project it onto the stage. There was *Dadaism*, which strung together nonsense words and phrases in a rebellion against the cold verbal logic that politicians used to justify bloodshed. There was *surrealism* and *symbolism* and *futurism* and almost too many other –isms to name. There was an interest in non-realistic Asian drama such as *noh* and *kabuki* and Chinese opera and some Western playwrights began combining these influences with their work. The work of Freud and Jung gave rise to an intense interest in the unseen psychological forces that drove characters.

In short, there was suddenly a multitude of ways of thinking about theatre, and the old convention that said that each play had one essential meaning no longer seemed to make much sense. In the face of so many options, the theatre began to demand not only someone who could stage plays realistically, but someone who could interpret them as well.

The range of options continues to expand today, as theatre is less guided by strict convention than at any point in history. Of course, the modern theatre is not entirely free of convention. We all agree (well, most of us) that cell-phones will be shut off at the start of a performance, and that the audience shouldn't attempt to talk to the performers (in many previous eras, shouting at the actors was expected and even encouraged). We agree that the house lights being lowered signals the start of a performance and that when they are raised the performance is over (again, for most of history the audience was as well lit as the performers). We expect a certain consistency of style within the same production. Yet these conventions are relatively simple, unrestrictive ones (and most of us are not shocked when any of these rules is artfully broken). The modern audience, who has the entire world literally at their fingertips via the Internet, and who has seen every manner of entertainment on their television sets and computer screens, is without a doubt the most open-minded the theatre has ever known. Because of that, we are perhaps more in need of the hand of the interpreter than ever before. With so many choices to make, someone has to make choices.

The Modern Director

How does one become a director? Many directors begin their careers as actors and actresses and then an opportunity presents itself and they realize that they have a penchant for working with actors, for coordinating the collaborators and for realizing a conceptual vision. Others work their way up theatre companies. Still others train via academic programs offered through universities with theatre as a liberal arts focus or through conservatories and specialized institutions. Graduate studies result in a master of fine arts in directing (MFA). Most graduate schools require some experience in directing before gaining admittance into a program. Once matriculated into a program, the directing student is able to study the many facets of theatre production, such as play analysis, history and theory, and acting techniques. Many programs require students to take classes in costume, set, and lighting design which help the director develop visual skills and a vocabulary necessary to communicate with the collaborators. Most MFA programs require at least a three-year commitment of study.

The Society of Stage Directors and Choreographers (SDC) is an independent national labor union that represents professional directors and choreographers who work in the theatre, and choreographers who work in the media. There are contracts for Broadway, Off- and Off-Off-Broadway, resident theatres, stock and dinner theatres, and special contracts for members working in college or university theatre programs and community theatres.

The Directing Process

Since the director is generally the single most influential artist involved in crafting the production, it is interesting that the directors' work is often the least obvious to a theatre audience. An audience will often leave a performance praising or criticizing the acting or the scenery or the costumes, but it is somewhat rarer for an audience to comment upon the direction. It is a paradox of the theatre: the director's work is often less visible because it is so pervasive—so intertwined with the work of every other artist. Even this brief list reveals how far-ranging and comprehensive are the director's responsibilities:

1. Selecting a script or agreeing to direct an offered script.
2. Reading the play (repeatedly, exhaustively) and decide on an interpretation and directorial concept for the production.
3. Casting the play via auditions and/or interviews.
4. Rehearsing with the actors, overseeing the staging and helping them understand and develop their characters.
5. Staging the production.
6. Collaborating with the costume, set, lighting, and sound designers and other theatre artists in order to unify all of the production elements into a cohesive and creative performance.

Script Selection

Not all directors are lucky enough to be able to select the play they direct. Many times, a director is hired by a producer or artistic director to direct a particular show. In cases where the director runs his or her own theatre, and in many college and university theatres, however, the director has more latitude. In these cases, a director is well-advised to choose a play with which she or he has a strong affinity. As we will see in the section on "Interpretation," it is the job of the director to "say something" with the play, and the more passionate he or she is about what that play has to say, the more powerful the production is likely to be. Most directors are avid play-readers, and they carry around in their heads a kind of "list" of plays they are yearning to direct. (In cases where the director does not choose the script, she or he must work more or less in reverse, seeking to *discover* a passion for the play.)

Many times, a director will be slated to direct a new play, one that has never before seen production or publication. In these cases, the play is often assumed to be less "finished," and so, in addition to normal directorial duties, the director is usually tasked with helping *develop* the play. The director will share with the playwright his or her insights about, say, the clarity of a character or the effectiveness of a particular scene. There is considerable give-and-take between the playwright and director and this process will continue into rehearsals with rewrites and revisions. Ideally this exchange of ideas is one of cooperation and mutual respect leading to a more cohesive script and thus a more cohesive production.

Whether or not the script is new, the first phase of the director's work is to explore and analyze the play to discover an interpretation, and to create a concept or directorial vision for the production.

Interpretation

Let us begin with a question: why does a play need interpretation at all? Won't the audience understand it just fine if it is presented "as is?" Why do we need some sort of "middleman" telling us what it's about? The answer is that one of our strongest present-day conventions is that a production present a unified vision of a play, and without a central interpretive artist, there exists the possibility that a production might take off in a hundred contradictory directions.

Even in a contemporary play—one in which the meaning seems fairly clear and obvious—there is the potential for wide disagreement between artists. For instance, many contemporary plays feature a blend of dark and comic elements, and absent an interpreter it may be difficult to decide how dark or how comic the production should be. If different actors held different views about the mood and atmosphere of the play, it is likely that actors in the same scene would seem to be acting in different plays. If the designers were similarly divided, then fanciful, whimsical costuming might end up illuminated by harsh or somber lighting (to the strains of creepy, unnerving music). If the play in question is one from a bygone era—such as the era of Shakespeare—the potential for disagreements about meaning dramatically increases.

So how does a director go about deciding on an interpretation? Sometimes there are external circumstances that may dictate (or at least color) an interpretation. If a historical drama was being presented by a community as part of an Independence Day celebration, then a sincere depiction of patriotism would likely be expected. If a Shakespeare play was being produced by a small experimental theatre, then the director would probably feel compelled to seek unique and surprising insights. It is in the many instances where the director has no constraints, however, where the process of deciding on an interpretation becomes most challenging—and most exhilarating.

The first thing a director does in crafting an interpretation is simply to read the text—repeatedly. In the time between play selection and auditions and rehearsals, a director must quite literally live with a script. During this period of exhaustive reading, the director asks questions of the play. What do I find most exciting about it? What does it seem to be "about?" What is the overriding mood of the piece? Is there a single theme that unites the many scenes? In answering these questions, the director begins, little by little, piece by piece, to put together what is known as a "production concept."

The term production concept simply refers to the particular interpretive slant a director applies to a play, but because there are so many different types of directors, using so many different approaches, these interpretive slants are framed in many different ways. Some directors are visual thinkers, and so they may tend to describe their production concepts using visual metaphors. For instance, a visually-minded director might tell her designers that the play is like "a beautiful flower breaking through sterile concrete" or "a fiery inferno." Such descriptions may sound like an odd way of approaching a text, but designers, being primarily visual artists, would probably find that they contained helpful suggestions about shapes and colors that might be used in the production.

Plays are stories, and stories consist of action. Someone desperately wants something, someone or something else is thwarting his or her desires, and the ensuing conflict is the core of the story. One of the early steps in interpretation involves figuring all of this out. Again, a series of questions must be asked and answered: Who is the central character (or protagonist)? What does this character want/need? Why does he or she need it? Who or what is getting in his or her way?

Sometimes, it is the action of the play that most informs the concept (see sidebar). The director will sometimes distill all of the major action of the play into a single action statement, commonly referred to as the spine of the play. The famous director and critic Harold Clurman, says the spine is the "fundamental drama or conflict" of which "the script's plot and people are instruments." As an example, in a play that featured ambitious characters in a cutthroat business environment, a director might decide that the ruling action is "clawing ones way to the top of the heap." A play about immigrants striking out to find new lives for themselves might feature the spine "to break free of stifling traditions." Directors who use this way of framing their interpretation say that it both helps them keep the play's action moving forward and gives the production a sense of cohesion and unity, since all of the different scenes must in some way serve the spine. Often directors will combine visual metaphor and spine, since metaphors usually contain some sense of the play's action. For instance, the flowers vs. concrete metaphor used above might nicely sum up the spine "to cast off the bonds of sterile conformity" or the fiery inferno might fit a spine such as "to purge the world of everything unclean."

It is worth mentioning that term *concept* is often misunderstood by the general public. Most of the time the word is used, it's used as criticism of a particularly bold interpretive choice: "Oh, it's *Hamlet* set during the Balkan War. I hate those *concept* productions!" In this reading of the term, concept solely refers to the director choosing a setting that may not have originally been envisioned by the playwright. As we have seen, however, *all* well-directed productions feature some kind of guiding interpretive vision, and so all could be said to be "concept productions."

On to some specific examples:

For Slippery Rock's 2008 production of *Macbeth*, the director's metaphor was "a tornado wherein Macbeth was sucked into the vortex only to be spit out into the chaos of fate." She focused on the destiny of fate as determined by the witches, who were embodied as *kabuki* and *noh* stylized dancers. The world of the play was a futuristic anarchy complemented by leather and steel and techno music. Shakespeare's text was also rearranged with some lines reassigned to different characters some of whom were also blended and morphed.

Orson Welles also directed a famous stage production of *Macbeth* in 1936. Welles set the play in an African jungle and used African-American actors in all of the roles. Known as the "voodoo *Macbeth*," the production was widely praised for its innovative treatment of Shakespeare's text, and is considered a landmark in African-American theatre history.

—David Skeele

In the 1948 film, directed by and starring Orson Welles, Shakespeare's text was rearranged but all the words were Shakespeare's. He conceived the play (in this case converted to a *screenplay*) in an antiquarian style, creating an eleventh-century Scottish moor with dark eaves and caves. The witches were mysterious hags. Macbeth's blind ambition was his ultimate ruin.

In 2008, Rupert Goold's *Macbeth* was transferred from the Chichester Festival in Great Britain to the Brooklyn Academy of Music, then to Broadway and finally as a BBC film. This *Macbeth* was set starkly in the Stalin era as imagined by George Orwell in *1984*. The joyless set felt like a morgue. The witches were hollow-eyed nurses. Patrick Stewart as Macbeth created a totalitarian dictator who descended into madness because of his hyperactive imagination.

These are only three of the countless conceptions and interpretations of Macbeth. As with any play, the potential for creativity is immeasurable, and that is why every production creates its own particular world of the play, some more successfully than others, but all striving for cohesiveness and unity of elements and style.

EXTRINSIC AND INTRINSIC INTERPRETATIONS

In simplest terms, an *intrinsic* production is one in which the director attempts to conform to what they believe to be the *intent* of the playwright. An *extrinsic* interpretation, on the other hand, is one in which the director intentionally creates something that clearly was not envisioned by the playwright. Generally, intrinsic interpretations are more likely to be found in productions of contemporary plays, while extrinsic interpretations are more often applied to classic plays.

These terms are far from clear-cut, however. As a playwright, I have sometimes had directors "see" something very clearly in one of my plays that I had never actually considered, and often I end up feeling that the unexpected choice works wonderfully onstage (and that it may have been "in" the play the whole time, whether or not I realized it). Was that choice, then, an intrinsic or extrinsic one? I'm not sure. Similarly, setting *King Lear* in a sterile government building in some distant Orwellian future sounds utterly extrinsic on the face of it, doesn't it? After all, Shakespeare could not possibly have imagined such a setting when he was writing the play. But what if this production was able to illuminate questions about power and authority and corruption that Shakespeare *did* intend, perhaps more brilliantly than a traditional production? Would it still be considered entirely extrinsic?

—David Skeele

The term *casting* comes from sculpture: to cast a mold, which is precisely what the director is doing during the audition process. The director is trying to fit the actor to the role. She is looking for the right combination of personality, energy, and physical appearance that will fulfill the vision of how a character is pictured in her mind. For larger endeavors, the director often works with a casting director to assist in the auditions and/or interviews. The casting director puts out a call to agents who submit headshots, resumes, or reels for consideration. Based on the parameters given by the director, the casting director chooses those actors who are most appropriate for each role and sets up an audition with the director.

> **CASTING**
> From a term used in sculpting; to cast a mold. In theatrical terms, this is the process through which the director and/or casting director fits the actor to the role, usually completed via auditions and callbacks where actors read with other actors to determine chemistry and sense of ensemble.

Auditions in professional theatre take several forms. In a "general audition," the actor usually presents one or two monologues of his own choosing. As the name implies, the purpose of this kind of audition is to give the director a general sense of the actor's ability. A general audition is often used as a kind of "elimination round," in which actors who are clearly unsuited to the roles in the play are weeded out. When actors make it through this round, they proceed to a phase of the auditions process referred to as "callbacks." There, they are given scripts (or short pieces of scripts, called "sides") and asked to read for specific roles. Sometimes the actor is given time to prepare for his reading, and sometimes he is simply given the sides and asked to read—this is what is known as a "cold reading."

In the university setting, auditions are usually open to all. Depending upon the number of people signed up, the director might hold a general audition or might proceed immediately to cold readings. After an evening of auditions, a callback list is posted (which usually lists which actors are called back for a particular role) and callbacks are scheduled. At this time, actors are given the opportunity to read with different combinations of actors for the director, who must decide which actors will create the most successful ensemble. There is a cliché in the theatre that claims "90% of directing is casting." This claim is of course a gross overstatement, one that undervalues the important work that takes place during rehearsals, but there is a shred of truth to it. Choosing talented, committed actors who are suitable for the roles—and who work well *together*—will make every other phase of the director's work much easier.

Typecasting happens when a director chooses actors because of their physical type and/or appearance. In past eras, it was established practice to divide actors into rigid character categories, and we still use much of the language of 18th-and 19th-century typecasters: i.e., leading lady, ingénue, character actor, etc. Typecasting is perhaps most prevalent in the professional theatre and in Hollywood, where the director is generally able to perfectly match casting requirements to available talent. In college and university theatre, however, the director's choices are more limited, and there are other sometimes other considerations that affect casting. College actors are *students*, and so must sometimes be given opportunities which allow them to grow and "stretch" their abilities by playing roles they might never be assigned in a professional setting. For instance, in a recent production of *The 25th Annual Putnam County Spelling Bee* one of the roles, a character named William Barfee, was described in the script as an overweight bully. Instead of casting an actor who fit that physical type, we cast an actor who was short and slight and used his intellect and emotional intensity rather than his physical size to bully the others. It was a highly original—and very effective—interpretation of the role. Such opportunities to work outside the bounds of type can be a vital part of the education of actors, helping them develop versatility. It is unlikely that a "chameleon" such as Johnny Depp ever would have attained his remarkable versatility without being given these kinds of challenges early in his career!

TYPECASTING

When an actor is chosen for a role based on physical type, appearance or personality. For example, Sylvester Stallone is cast more successfully in roles where he plays the tough guy: the boxer, the soldier, the action hero. Johnny Depp is never type-cast! He is a chameleon who has the talent to morph into any role from Captain Jack Sparrow to Willy Wonka.

Currently, there exists a trend in theatre called non-traditional or "color-blind" casting. This means that the director casts the best actor for the role regardless of color, and that the audience will respond to the character rather than the actor's race (even when actors of different ethnicities play members of the same family). As the world becomes more diverse and socially aware, this trend will serve as a way of expressing and addressing the diversity of the U.S. population.

—Laura Smiley

As the director is preparing the text and choosing the performers, she is simultaneously working with her other collaborators: the designers of the set, lights, costumes, and sound to develop the visual and aural aspects of the production. This is where directorial concept is crucial in communicating what the director envisions as the world of the play. The director and designers must work closely together to ensure that the acting style will mesh with the above elements and vice versa.

Famed British director Jonathan Miller offers a fascinating idea about when it is appropriate to shift a play out of its original timeframe (and when it is not). In his view, after a certain amount of time has passed, a play enters what he calls its "after-life"—a period in which the playwright's original intentions can no longer be well understood by the present culture. The plays of Shakespeare, he argues, contain many ideas and images and feelings that we would regard as "universal," but they also contain so many Elizabethan references and reflect so much of an Elizabethan understanding of history, science, geography, etc., that a modern audience cannot possibly understand them in the same way the original audience did. Thus, Miller believes, modern directors have an obligation to explore and illuminate modern perspectives on Shakespeare's plays. The same would not be true, however, of a play written in, say, the twentieth century. Since twenty-first-century audiences would still be able to fully understand the playwright's intentions, Miller argues that the director then has more of an obligation to honor those intentions.

—David Skeele

The rehearsal process for the play begins in the weeks before the first public performance of the play. It is during this time that the director works most intensely with the actors. On the first day of rehearsal, most directors give a speech to the company describing the play and the approach to be taken to interpret and stage the text. At this time, designers will usually present drawings and models to the cast. If the production features a *dramaturg*, then research about the play's historical period or production history may be presented. A readthrough and discussion generally follow, in which actors may voice questions about plot and meaning and character interpretation. Some directors will continue reading and discussing for several days (a process called "table work"); others will break away from the conference table at the first opportunity and begin the process that usually forms the bulk of the director's rehearsal work: staging.

Staging

Staging, in its simplest definition, means determining where and when the actors move. It is one of the most crucial parts of the directing process. Stage a production well, and it will be clear and exciting and fun to look at; stage it poorly and the end result will likely be confusing and static and dull. Why is staging so important? Let's take a look at a few of the reasons:

Staging Creates Visual Variety

Let's face it, audiences—especially 21st-century audiences—are easily bored. Where Shakespeare's audience—accustomed to standing and listening to three- or four-hour religious sermons—was an audience of *listeners*, the experience of the modern audience has been shaped by endless time spent viewing movie, television and computer screens. We are a *visual* culture, and so in order to hold our interest we need a stage picture that shifts and moves and changes. If a director simply placed four actors in chairs side by side and asked them to speak the lines for two hours—no matter how fine the writing, no matter how emotionally intense the acting—most audience members would go mad with boredom.

Staging Tells the Story

Imagine a short snippet of a dramatic scene, one in which a husband of many years tells his wife "You have deceived and humiliated me for the last time!" Now imagine four possible ways of making this happen onstage. 1) The husband and wife stand at opposite sides of the stage, staring at each other. 2) The husband hurls a chair to the floor on the line, then storms out, slamming the door as he goes. 3) The husband approaches the wife slowly on the line, reaching into his coat pocket as does. 4) The husband delivers the line, starts to run offstage, then runs back and falls to his knees in front of the wife. What do the different staging interpretations tell you about the husband? The wife? The story? In version 1, the story is the least definite, the most mysterious. The husband and wife would seem to be of more or less equal power, and there is the sense of a challenge being laid down. What will happen? The ambiguity of the staging piques our interest. In version 2, the husband is clearly distraught, and he seems to have ceded much of the power in the relationship to the wife (notice that *he* leaves—if he had remained and forced her to leave it would have said something entirely different). Version 3 is menacing, scary. The husband has all of the power, and he seems ready to use it in some destructive way. In version 4, the husband is completely powerless, held in the thrall of the wife. He can't even make an angry statement without collapsing and begging forgiveness.

How could these simple changes in staging tell such entirely different stories? The answer is that while words are one thing we use to communicate, they are *only* one thing. Physical movement—whether large movements such as a dramatic exit or small movements such as fidgeting or sagging or displaying anxious body language—is what gives our words context. Without the context of the actors' movement, it becomes much harder for the audience to understand what is going on.

Staging Provides Focus

When it comes to the issue of audience focus, the film director has it easy. With each camera shot, she has determined for the audience exactly where it should be looking. If she wants us to take in the whole panorama of an outdoor scene, she uses a long shot. If she wants us now to focus on the inner anguish of the lead character, she zooms in his face, perhaps even just on his eyes. If it becomes important for us to see another character reacting to that anguish, she simply switches cameras and shows us the other character.

The theatre director values the ability to focus the audience nearly as much as the film director, but how does he control it, when the theatre audience is free to look wherever it wants? The answer is staging.

There are a number of staging methods a director uses to steer audience focus from one part of the stage to another. For instance, our eyes tend to be attracted to elements that are *different* from the rest of the stage picture. If most of the cast is dancing an energetic waltz, then our eyes will be drawn to the solitary figure sitting motionless in the center of the action. Contrastingly, if there is a restaurant scene with groups of people talking quietly at tables, we be irresistibly pulled toward the stranger who enters with a frenetic energy and bustles about the room. If most of the cast is clumped together at one end of the stage, we'll be most interested in the person who stands alone at the other end. Sometimes directors use the focus of the other actors to control the audience's focus. If everyone onstage turns to look at a particular character, so will everyone in the audience. Often, a director will discover that there are certain places on the set that draw focus—i.e., a high platform, or a clear area completely unobstructed by furniture—and into these spots he will endeavor to maneuver the appropriate character at the appropriate time.

Staging Clarifies Where the Action Changes

Most of us have had, at one time or another, the unfortunate experience of seeing productions that seem to play on one monotonous level. Whether that one level is listless droning or passionate yelling, unvarying theatre quickly becomes unbearable. Thus, one of the most important jobs the director and the actors have is to discover where the scenes and the characters *change*. Staging is the best of way of making these moments—which we call "beat changes"—clear to the audience, and also of making them clear to the actor.

As an example, think of the moment in version 4 of our imaginary scene-snippet where the husband decides he cannot leave his wife, no matter how badly she may have treated him. It's a classic beat-change moment, as the character changes action (from spurning his wife to begging her to take him back) and emotion (from anger to despair). If the director allowed that moment to happen while the husband sat in a chair next his wife, he would risk it passing unnoticed by the audience, and unfelt by the actor. However, remember how we staged it: the character starts for the door, freezes, then swivels back and throws himself at her feet. The action would be eminently clear to every audience member (even if there were no words at all), and no actor could execute that movement without feeling the impact of those changes.

German playwright, poet and novelist Johann Wolfgang von Goethe was invited in 1775 to oversee the court theatre in Weimar in Germany. At this point he was quite famous and at first didn't take his duties seriously. By the 1790s he had become a *regisseur*, or a dictatorial director. He had become enthusiastic about the theatre and had high expectations of his actors. He had lengthy rehearsal periods and expected his actors to work as an ensemble. He instituted uniform stage speech rather than a variety of dialects, and also established rules for stage movement (as well as rules for the performers' behavior in their personal lives!). He emphasized careful stage composition creating pictorial arrangements of actors on stage, and he also oversaw settings and costumes, for which he endeavored to apply historical accuracy. Our modern tradition of audience decorum can be traced back to Goethe who had rules even for the audience. Appropriate audience reactions were either applause, or attentive silence.

—Laura Smiley

Directing Styles

Since every director is a unique individual artist, there could be said to be as many directing styles as there are directors. Some are highly visual, and place a premium on the appearance of the costumes and sets and the overall attractiveness of the stage picture. Others are far more interested in the emotionality of the play and focus most of their attention on the actors. Some are warm and empathetic, some are cold and cynical. Some find humor in the darkest of dramas, others see the darkness in the most frivolous comedies. As with all artists, directors are influenced in everything they do by their upbringing, their experiences, their political beliefs, perhaps even their genetics.

Within all of these variables, however, it is possible to loosely identify some prevalent directorial styles. Directing style is usually defined in terms of how much or how little freedom the director allows the other artists involved with the production. At one side of the spectrum is what is known as the *dictatorial* director. To this type of director (at least in the extreme version), the actors are little more than puppets. When it comes to staging, for instance, the dictatorial director will spend untold hours with a model of the set and little cardboard figures of the characters, plotting out every movement in every scene before she hears the actors speak a word. The movement will be taught to the actors over the first week or so of rehearsal, and then run repeatedly until the director's vision is perfectly realized. Generally, an extremely dictatorial director will be equally unyielding with designers (see the chapter on "The Rehearsal Process" for a more detailed discussion of the director/designer relationship).

At the other end of the spectrum exists what is called the *organic* director. In the extreme version, this type of director does very little in the way of decision-making, preferring to allow the other artists to "discover" what is in the play by following their own instincts. When staging a scene, he will answer the question "where do I move?" with "where do you want to move?" This type of director could be said to be less a director than a "creative coordinator."

The extremes of both types are usually problematic in practice. When actors have little or no input into the creative process, such lack of investment may be apparent in their work. The performances may lack passion and the excitement of discovery. Contrastingly, when actors have little or no direction, focus and storytelling clarity often suffer, making the production feel somewhat random and formless.

Fortunately, few directors live at the extreme edges of this spectrum. Most find a way of combining their predetermined vision of the play with the new discoveries of the other artists (while remaining open to their own new discoveries). Rather than being a dictator or a coordinator, this type functions as a kind of *guide* or helmsman. Though still guided by a strong interpretation, she will use rehearsals and design conferences to provoke and stimulate the actors and designers. This director creates an atmosphere in which actors dig, probe, and investigate the whole fabric of the play. The directorial concept precedes the first day's work, but the "sense of direction" only crystallizes into a consistent stage image as the process nears an end.

Conclusion

While the role of the director is a relatively new development in theatre practice, the modern director makes a valuable contribution to the process of making meaning in the theatre. Building on the contributions of forerunners of the modern theatre, the director organizes the casting, rehearsal, and production process. The director also creates an interpretation and communicates a conceptual vision to other collaborators in a production.

Suggested Exercises

- Develop a production concept for the play you have selected.
- Create a one-page handout that identifies your concept.
- Select a scene to stage (two to three minutes). Block the scene in a way that expresses your interpretation.
- Select volunteers from the class (or outside of the class with approval of the course instructor) to serve as actors for the scene/monologue. You must incorporate at least one rehearsal technique into your workshop.
- Schedule a class time to workshop your scene/monologue with your actors for the class.
- You will be evaluated on your written component and the successful completion of your performance component as scheduled.

ACTORS

Laura Smiley

CHAPTER OBJECTIVES

- Identify the role of the actor in making meaning in the theatre.
- Understand the steps in the audition process.
- Distinguish between the internal and external approach to acting.
- Recognize the contribution of Konstantin Stanislavski to contemporary acting methods and understand the fundamentals of the steps in his system.
- Identify the contributions of the Group Theatre to the American Acting Method, including the techniques of Lee Strasberg and Stella Adler.

KEY TERMS

Affective memory
Cattle call
Improvisation
Monologue
Subtext

The title of a popular television show, *Whose Line Is it Anyway?*, focuses on witty and hilarious improvisational situations and showcases just one of the many skills that need to be continually developed and honed by both aspiring and seasoned actors. But to ask the question, "Whose line is it anyway?" is just the tip of the iceberg of what the actor's process entails. Frequently, my beginning acting students see a play and ask in wonder, "How do they learn all those lines?" I can guarantee that while memorization is certainly key to performing the role, there is much more to the process, and within that, there are tools utilized to develop the characters which ultimately also help the actor to learn her lines!

Those tools come into play long before an actor is actually cast in a play. Let's take some time to consider just what it takes to prepare. "Prepare for what?" you ask. The audition! The audition is the equivalent of a job interview, although the actor usually has only two to three minutes to prove that she should be considered for the callbacks. Acting is a highly competitive profession. There are many more actors and aspiring actors than roles available at every level: Broadway, regional theatres, universities, training programs, even community theatres.

To be prepared for the audition, the actor should have a portfolio of **monologues** that she can access on a moment's notice. Auditioning is a skill on its own. Auditioning can be nerve-wracking. You are putting yourself on display and are being judged on whether or not you can act! Actors love to perform in plays. I always tell my students that rather than feeling like you are being judged, think of it as an opportunity to do your one-person play! You have done the prep work just as you do for a play and this is your chance to show them what you've got!

Andy Allison in *Cabaret*, directed by Laura Smiley for the Slippery Rock University Theatre Department, 2009.

MONOLOGUE

One to three minutes of memorized text that are performed solo. Actors should have in their portfolios a selection of contrasting monologues: a comedic piece, a dramatic piece, and one or more serio-comic pieces from contemporary plays; and contrasting classical texts, at least one of which should come from the works of Shakespeare. Actors need to choose pieces that show their range and flexibility while also being age-appropriate and creative. There are monologues that should be avoided as well—pieces that are overdone, like Helena in *A Midsummer Night's Dream*. Often, actors take an auditioning class or work with a coach to help them choose monologues and prepare.

So, you have your monologues ready, what do you do next? Find auditions! Auditions are posted in various ways. In New York there is a newspaper called *Backstage* which is published every week. Actors can check the Equity call-boards and hotline, and numerous websites. For graduate programs there are the University/Resident Theatre Association's auditions (URTAs) as an option to be seen by many schools at once. In Pittsburgh notices are posted at universities, the *Pittsburgh Post Gazette* (in the Weekend section) and the *City Paper*. At universities, watch for posters and e-mail announcements. Send in a headshot (an 8x10 photo and resume), call for an appointment, show up for the **cattle call**.

CATTLE CALL

Also called an *open call audition*, this gives hundreds, sometimes thousands, of performers the opportunity to be seen for a limited number of roles, like when *American Idol* searches for contestants. If *Grease* were being cast, hundreds of young men would show up in leather jackets and ducktails. In reality, the chances of winning a major role this way are slim but there's always a success story of the director who took a chance and found a diamond in the rough.

You make the appointment and choose a monologue or two that's most fitting for the play you are auditioning for, and you audition. You have four minutes, and in those four minutes you must show your understanding of the text and character, your stage presence, and your power to reach an audience. You must jump into the role at performance energy without aid of a costume or set or other actors; your passion must shine through! And...you did it! You've been called back for another round of auditions! What happens next?

This is where it can get interesting. Callbacks happen in a myriad of ways depending on the director, the production, and the production company. Some auditions can focus on cold readings of the play about to be produced. Actually, sometimes this happens at the initial audition. If possible, I suggest to my actors that they read the play they are auditioning for. There are several reasons why this is a helpful step: to choose the monologues that are most appropriate, to have an idea of what role you may be considered for, and to be familiar with the play should a cold reading occur. A cold reading happens when the actor is given a scene from the play and has minimal time to prepare. He must read from the script with a stage manager or member of the staff, neither of whom are actors. At callbacks there may be interviews, improvisations, and several readings with other potential cast members for the director to get a sense of what you can do and how she will form an ensemble for the play. And then...you wait for the call.

BRAVO! The call has come! You are cast! You are now about to embark on the rehearsal process, an exciting time of discovery! Actors do many things to prepare for their roles. They read histories of their characters or of the time period, or both. They study real-life situations, for instance, shadowing a nurse on her rounds. Actors may immerse themselves in the circumstances of their characters' lives before trying to interpret them for the stage. Sometimes actors will transform themselves, gaining or losing weight, coloring their hair, working out intensively to achieve a new body shape, or learning new skills like playing the piano or juggling. And all this can happen before the first day of rehearsal!

What is true for all actors is that to create the character one needs to have a tremendous work ethic. First of all, you explore with the ensemble your characters and their relationships with openness and receptiveness to each other and the director. You try different staging ideas or blocking (life-like patterns of movement in most cases) which are tested and then often discarded. You discover the rhythm of a scene and the pace at which it should be played. You must be rested and prepared for each day's work. At each rehearsal you must be prepared to try new blocking and different line readings, and be willing and able to repeat a sword fight over and over to get it right or whatever it takes to make that love scene work.

Often in rehearsal there is **improvisation**, sometimes abbreviated as *improv*, a useful tool to make real imaginative situations and to make imaginative situations real.[1] Improvisation can be used as a warm-up or to explore and create backstories for the characters or to solve acting or blocking problems.

IMPROVISATION
Spontaneous invention that goes beyond the scripted material to explore aspects of character or situation.[2]

In acting classes we so often refer to what we do as our "work." And sometimes this refers to something heavy and ponderous. *Theatre Games* help us remember that a play is called just that; a play. And play is sometimes left out of our work as actors. Theatre Games help us to remember the value of spontaneity and the beauty of the unknown. They allow us to explore a situation unhampered by the demands of a script, and they can reconnect us to our fellow actors.[3]

Viola Spolin is considered the mother of improvisation. She developed her Theatre Games from Neva Boyd, who worked in Chicago with the city's poorest children at Hull House. What Boyd discovered was that when she led these children in imaginative games their spirits soared, as well as their expressive freedom. Spolin took her teachings one step further. She was familiar with Konstantin Stanislavski's system and the way it was being taught in the United States and she felt that the work was all too serious and without joy. Grown-ups now that they were "grown up" had abandoned playing! She organized a group of actors in Chicago and began "playing" with possibility. One of the actors was her son Paul Sills, who later founded the Compass Theatre which then became The Second City, the famous improv troupe. That Spolin is the mother of improvisation is no understatement!

At the beginning of this chapter I referred to the development of the character as a key component of the actor's process. Now that you have been cast, how do you develop a character? There are two distinct schools of thought: the internal and the external approach. The mind or the body. The physical or the psychological. Throughout different periods of time one or the other has prevailed. In the twentieth century, physical acting was the preferred technique of the British, while the psychological technique prevailed in America.

Internal/External Approach

If you were to approach your character from an internal perspective, you would focus on the psychological aspects of your character, identifying areas of the character's life that correspond with your own experiences of life. This internal approach is associated with the teachings of *Konstantin Stanislavski* (more on his system later!). You would draw on your reactions to situations and your personal history to inform the life of the character you are creating. Very often, actors who work this way construct an autobiography of the character, a life and backstory beyond what the playwright has given them in the text. They look for deep motivations and objectives to discover what drives their characters to do what they do in any given moment of the play. They delve into their past to create emotional responses which they then transfer to the lives of their characters. They make use of **subtext**, which is the underlying thoughts behind or between lines—thus the phrase "read between the lines." These thoughts are unspoken but can be clearly communicated by how the line is spoken, physicalized or facially expressed.

Alexis Stanford in *As You Like It*, directed by Laura Smiley for the Slippery Rock University Theatre Department, 2008.

SUBTEXT
The underlying thoughts behind or between an actor's lines.

Think for example of how many ways you might express "Gee, great haircut!" The actors explore the reasons why their characters do what they do, what influences their behavior and ask the question "What would I do if I were this character in this situation?" The physicalization of the character follows the psychological exploration and expresses the character's mental state. This is working from the inside out.

In contrast, the external or technical approach is working from the outside in; that is, working with tools outside the realm of the psychological. It uses the imagination to find a physical manifestation of the character: how she walks, talks, gestures. If you were to approach your character from an external perspective you might first analyze the language: how you speak the text, interpret a line, taste the words.

Actors who work this way access emotion through their expressive abilities rather than through an emotional response. They explore the cadence and rhythm of the words as well as the physical manifestations of the body through gesture and posture. Frequently the physical life can unleash an emotional response. Just as the psychological actor finds an external physicalization, the physical actor is also aware of the motivations and objectives, the wants and needs, of his character.

Many training programs today meld the two approaches together to create an integration of style which I believe is the most effective and affective method of creation. Depending on the role one may choose one or the other as a start-

Andy Allison in *Cabaret*, directed by Laura Smiley for the Slippery Rock University Theatre Department, 2009.

ing point but in the end, there needs to be a synthesis of mind and body to create a vibrant and believable character.

In rehearsal a crucial part of the work is to discover action and reaction. In performance, this entails listening to the other actors on stage and reacting as if you were hearing these lines for the very first time. It involves creating the atmosphere and environment of the play: feeling the chill of the cold or the heat of the summer; the emptiness of a room or the feeling of a crowded room. When you act and react on stage the most important thing you create is the believability of your character in response to the other characters embodying the world of the play. This is the actor's charge to "be in the moment."

How does one "be in the moment"? By doing the things I've just described, by taking apart the text and putting it back together. Kathleen Chalfant, perhaps best known for her portrayal of Vivian Bearing, a character dying of cancer in the Pulitzer Prize-winning play *Wit* by Margaret Edson, sums it up like this: "In order to act you must take apart something that happens faster than thought, break it into component parts, and then put it back together. That's also what rehearsal is, breaking down a speech or reaction, and then getting it close to the speed at which a human being actually does it. Quite often, plays are just a little slower than life because you've added a step, the breaking down. The trick is to act as quickly as you think, which is not necessarily a function of speed. When you're doing it properly, it often feels as though you have all the time in the world. Then you can allow yourself to be entirely taken, with no conscious control. That's being in the moment, you have to have done all the work beforehand: knowing the words backwards and forwards, knowing where you're supposed to stand, and more importantly, knowing what the character is doing at every turn and why she does it."[4]

Stanislavski

The path to becoming an actor is paved in many different ways but all require the knowledge of technique and talent. *Konstantin Stanislavski* actively researched and developed the Stanislavski System in the early twentieth century. His work was ever evolving.

Stanislavski was the cofounder of the Moscow Art Theatre and the first director of Anton Chekhov's plays. In the late nineteenth century the trend in plays was called realism, that is everyday characters and situations close to real life. Stanislavski is considered the first theatre practitioner because he studied, compiled and codified a series of techniques and principles used to train actors in the creation of real believable characters on stage.

It seems a simple task; to act believably on stage, simply be natural. But Stanislavski discovered that this was not the case. It was extremely difficult to be convincing on stage. He went so far as to say that actors needed to reeducate themselves. In *An Actor Prepares* he writes, "All of our acts, even the simplest, which are so familiar to us in everyday life, become strained when we appear behind the footlights...before a public of a thousand people. That is why it is necessary to correct ourselves and learn again how to walk, sit or lie down. It is essential to reeducate ourselves to look and see, on the stage, to listen and to hear."[5] Because Stanislavski was an actor, he was directly involved in this development of a realistic approach. By studying the great actors of his day, Eleanora Duse and Tommaso Salvini among others, as well as observing himself, he was able to identify what these great actors did naturally and intuitively.

The foundation of his thinking lies in this: Stanislavski said, "The actor must first of all believe in everything that takes place on stage and most of all, he must believe what he himself is doing. And one can only believe in the truth." (*An Actor's Handbook* by Constantin Stanislavski. Routledge (2004), p. 126.) In order to quantify this foundation, Stanislavski studied how people acted in everyday situations, how their feelings and emotions were communicated and then he found ways to accomplish the same things on stage. These observations resulted in a series of exercises and techniques for the actor, which had the following broad aims:

1. To make the outward behavior of the performer—gestures, voice, and rhythm of movements—natural and convincing.
2. To have the actor or actress convey the goals and objectives—the inner needs—of a character. Even if all the physical manifestations are mastered, a performance will appear superficial and mechanical without a deep sense of conviction and belief.
3. To make the life of the character on stage not only dynamic but continuous. Some performers tend to emphasize only the high points of a part; in between the life of the character stops. In real life, however, people do not stop living.
4. To develop a strong sense of ensemble playing with other performers in a scene.[6]

Let us now explore the techniques that propel the above aims of the actor in creating a character. Following is an overview of the fruits of his labor.

Relaxation

It is impossible to tell someone to simply relax. And actually total relaxation is not the ultimate goal. What we are looking for is the release of unnecessary tension in the voice and body. This can be achieved via physical and vocal exercises. For example: stand with your feet hip width apart. Take a deep breath and roll down your spine. Shake your arms loose from your body, swinging your arms side to side like a rag doll. Slowly and with awareness, roll up the spine vertebra by vertebra, head and neck being the last to come up. With a continued sense of awareness scan through your body and tense the muscles in your feet then release them. Moving up the leg, tense your calves and release them, tense and release the thigh muscles, and slowly work up your body tensing and releasing. This is one of many exercises that are useful as a warm-up before performing on stage. Actually, once on stage one can have the awareness on mind and body while acting. Stanslavski speaks of a duality of presence on stage: there is the character and the actor.

Concentration and Observation

Stanislavski also discovered that gifted performers always appeared fully concentrated on some object, person or event while onstage. Stanislavski referred to the extent or range of concentration as the *circle of attention*. This circle of attention can be compared to a circle of light on a darkened stage. The performer should begin with the idea that it is a small tight circle including only himself or herself and perhaps one other person or one piece of furniture. When the performer has established a strong circle of attention, he or she can enlarge the circle outward to include the entire stage area. In this way performers will stop worrying about the audience and lose their self-consciousness.[7]

The Magic "If"

Stanislavski says the word "if" propels the imagination towards opening doors. It's not simply what would I do "if" I were this person. One must be more specific to avoid acting in a generalized fashion. What would I do if I were this character in this situation? Your imagination, activated by the magic "if," is what enables you to enter the imaginary given circumstances of the play without violating your sense of truth.

Deb Cohen in *As You Like It*, directed by Laura Smiley for the Slippery Rock University Theatre Department, 2008.

A simple exercise to illustrate the power of given circumstances.

A. Yes.

B. No.

A. Why?

B. Because.

A. When.

B. Soon

The given circumstances are that the characters are a mother and young son. They are in the car. The boy has to go to the bathroom.

Next try this one: The given circumstances are that the characters are a young couple. The young lady would like to get married. The gentleman is avoiding the subject.

Given Circumstances

These are the *who, what, where, when, why,* and *how* given by the playwright and further illuminated by the actor.

Actions and Objectives Onstage

The *what, why, and how* further defined. Actions are used to move a character's *objective* forward. Actions are tactics, the *how* you reach or attain an objective. An objective is what the character really wants. Acting is doing, according to Stanislavski. What you do are actions, and every action must have a purpose. This is also called the *psychophysical action*. A student at one of Stanislavski's lectures in 1917 noted the change in viewpoint from Stanislavski: "Whereas action previously had been taught as the expression of a previously-established "emotional state," it is now action itself which predominates and is the key to the psychological."[8]

Andy Allison in *Cabaret*, directed by Laura Smiley for the Slippery Rock University Theatre Department, 2009.

It is these physical actions that must be connected in concert with the circumstances to create the character's reality which is governed by the character's overall objective in the play. In the early twentieth century when Stanislavksi first started researching acting techniques, he focused on the inner aspects of training: what emotional experiences from the actor's unconscious could be remembered, mined and usedto connect and create a character's inner life. This is also called **affective memory**. Lee Strasberg, whom we will read about later, focused on this controversial technique as the basis of his Method.

Through-Line of a Role

The actor's question when analyzing a role: what does the character want above all else during the course of the play? What is the superobjective? What drives the character forward? This *superobjective* is the ultimate goal which is reached via the through-line of the character. This through-line is like a series of guideposts, that leads the character from immediate objectives to main objectives within each scene until the end of the play when the superobjective is finally realized or not. It is important to note here that not all actions and objectives carry the same weight of importance. All are not created equal! If you put too much emphasis on a minor objective or action, it will hurt the overall structure of your character. It will weaken the importance of the superobjective.

Ensemble and Communion

The definition for *ensemble* is something like this: a group of complementary parts working together as a unit. Ensemble in acting is the playing together of all the performers, how they connect and affect each other on stage, how each actor is a cog in the wheel without which the wheel wouldn't go round.

Andy Allison and Stacie O'Hara in *Cabaret*, directed by Laura Smiley for the Slippery Rock University Theatre Department, 2009.

BRESTOFF OBSERVES

This is a crucial part of Stanislavski's system. The living exchange between the characters in a scene, the communion between them is what rivets the audience's attention. The completeness of that communion helps each individual in the auditorium forget himself and enter into the drama on stage. This is another kind of communion; the audience with the characters, with the story.[8] This whole system of Stanislavski's is the most complete and practical yet devised for the training of an actor. It is designed to create that receptive shore over which inspiration can flow. It does not promise however to make you a great actor. According to Stanislavski acting cannot be taught. His method is a means not an end. It is meant to keep falseness and cliché out of the theatre. It is meant to transport the audience into the reality of the imagination; to take them out of the theatre and into the world of the characters. With the result that a mutual and beautiful communal act of the imagination takes place between the author, the actors and the audience.[10]

The American Method

Stanislavski's teachings have influenced the training of twentieth-century actors around the world. We will focus on the American Revolution of his work and the teachers who interpreted his techniques and made them their own. The Moscow Art Theatre performed in New York City in January of 1923, took the city by storm, and inspired many young actors to dedicate their training to this new kind of theatre. In May of 1930, twenty-seven actors and three others set out to rehearse in a barn in Connecticut and create Moscow Art Theatre American-style! This was the Group Theatre. Much of American training in Stanislavski's acting methods today came out of the Group experience. Innovators included Lee Strasberg, Stella Adler and Sanford Meisner, whose methodologies we will explore below.

Lee Strasberg became one of the best known acting teachers in America. He would transform the Stanislavski System to his American "Method." He explained his approach this way:

> *The human being who acts is the human being who lives. That is a terrifying circumstance. Essentially the actor acts a fiction, a dream; in life the stimuli to which we respond are always real. The actor must constantly respond to stimuli that are imaginary. And yet this must happen not only just as it happens in real life, but actually more fully and more expressively. Although the actor can do things in life quite easily, when he has to do the same thing on the stage under fictitious conditions he has difficulty because he is not equipped as a human being merely to playact at imitating life. He must somehow believe. He must somehow be able to convince himself of the rightness of what he is doing in order to do things fully on the stage.[11]*

As referred to earlier, Stanislavski developed the technique of *emotional recall* or affective memory early in his career. Strasberg focused his teachings around this technique which at first was heralded among those at the Group Theatre and then later became the subject of great dispute amongst them. In 1947, members of the Group Theatre started the Actors Studio in New York City as a workshop where actors could work out their problems away from the pressures of commercial theatre. Strasberg, the Actor's Studio, and the Method are almost synonymously linked. And Strasberg's Method has stirred up some of the most passionate arguments about modern acting in the twentieth century. This Method is a version of Stanislavski that focuses on affective memory, or the inner workings of emotional response in order to express deep feelings when needed.

Strasberg interpreted *emotional recall* as the actor's conscious efforts to remember circumstances surrounding an emotion-filled occasion from the past in order to stimulate impulses and emotions that could be used on stage. The actor recreates in the mind's eye all of the surrounding circumstances, the sensory and emotional detail that were part of the remembered experience.[12]

> It must be noted there is a difference between affective memory and emotional recall however. The basic idea of affective memory is not emotional recall but that the actor's emotion on the stage should never be real. It always should be only remembered emotion. An emotion that happens right now is out of control...Remembered emotion is something that the actor can create and repeat: without that the thing is hectic.[13]

So, if affective memory is not feeling the real emotion on the stage in the moment, how do you do that? Remember Pavlov's dogs? They were conditioned to salivate at the sound of a bell whether food was present or not. So can emotions be conditioned? By recreating the physical circumstances the sense memory of an event, the emotions can be accessed. So, the actor does not focus on feeling the emotion but on the physical surroundings of the event.

So that's great for accessing emotions, but how does that actually work in a scene? The actor finds affective memory that closely mirrors the emotion needed in a scene. He does exercises to access this emotion until he can do it in a minute with the words and actions of the scene. He doesn't use words at first, but slowly builds up the memory and adds the words in with practice. And this is where the great controversy arises.

Stanislavski realized the value of these affective memory exercises, but in later years he felt that putting too great an emphasis on feeling led the actor astray. Wasn't this like dropping out of the moment in order to do an exercise to access an emotion?

Well, it doesn't really matter if the moment being acted out is a close-up in a film. Many actors have found the greatest use of affective memory is before a camera. For take after take, this exercise can be tremendously useful. When the camera is focused mostly, or exclusively, on one actor, that one actor needn't worry about the connection with his scene partner. In such a situation, it is the believability of the emotion that is paramount. And so it is here, that affective memory really comes into its own.[14]

This is perhaps why so many Actors Studio actors are so successful on film. Famous students include Paul Newman, Robert DeNiro, and Al Pacino. However, a link often mistakenly connected lies between Strasberg, and Marlon Brando and his genius (or mumblings.) First of all, Strasberg never taught Marlon Brando.

Here is what Brando has to say about Strasberg in his 1994 autobiography: "Lee Strasberg tried to take credit for teaching me how to act. He never taught me anything...To me he was a tasteless and untalented person...I went to the Actors Studio...because of Elia Kazan...But Strasberg never taught me acting. Stella did."[15]

Yes, Stella Adler. Her work is very often contrasted with the teachings of Strasberg. Whereas Strasberg was focused on the actor's emotional life as it relates to creating feelings on stage, Adler focused on the creation of character on stage. Like Stanislavski, Adler focused on imagination, actions, and circumstances. Although she was an original member of the Group Theatre, she was ambivalent about it from the beginning and she was rather suspicious of Strasberg's technique of affective memory. As an actress she was perfectly capable of allowing the situation to carry her in the moment, and felt that delving into one's personal life for memories was invasive. In July of 1934 Adler met Konstantin Stanislavski in Paris. He was there recuperating from an illness and she had been travelling in Russia with Group leader Harold Clurman observing different theatres. When they heard Stanislavski was in Paris, they decided to visit him.

At the time, Adler was in rehearsal under Strasberg. His dictatorial style was getting under her skin and the affective memory exercises were no longer working for her at all. She lost all joy in acting. She blamed Stanislavski's system for this change...and then her world exploded!

Stanislavski said if the system made her lose all the joy she had for acting, then the system was not for her. But then he suggested that perhaps she wasn't using the system the right way. She told him of the work the Group Theatre was doing and when she talked about affective memory exercises, Stanislavski stopped her and said that he had abandoned that teaching years ago because it led to hysteria in the actors! For six weeks they worked many hours into the night. For Stella it was a revelation! She couldn't wait to share her learning with the Group!

It is important to note that an actor may be well trained, competent, and successful, but there is another key ingredient that must be present to make a performance electrifying. This is the acting that cannot be taught. It happens when a performer connects with the audience in a palpable kinesthetic manner. How to describe it? Charisma, presence, personality...it's truly difficult to describe but you know it when you see it!

Conclusion

This chapter has outlined the role of the actor in making meaning in the theatre from the audition to the rehearsal process to the performance. Much of today's acting method can be traced to the work of Russian actor Konstantin Stanislavski who developed a system of character development based on internal and external approaches. In the United States we have adapted many of Stanislavski's theories into the American Method. Lee Strasberg and Stella Adler continue to influence today's actors on stage and film.

Endnotes

[1] *The Creative Spirit* by Stephanie Arnold. McGraw-Hill Higher Education, (2008), p. 143

[2] Ibid.

[3] *The Great Acting Teachers and Their Methods* by Richard Brestoff. Smith and Kraus Books,(1995), p. 146.

[4] Kathleen Chalfant quoted in Janet Sonnenberg, *The Actor Speaks*. New York: Random House, (1990), p. 252.

[5] *An Actor Prepares* by Konstantin Stanislavski. New York: Theatre Arts, (1948), p73.

[6] *The Theatre Experience*, 10th Edition by Edwin Wilson. McGraw-Hill Higher Education, (2007), pp. 129–30.

[7] *The Theatre Experience*, 10th Edition by Edwin Wilson. McGraw-Hill Higher Education, (2007), p. 130.

[8] *Stanislavski* by Jean Benedetti. New York: Routledge, (1988), p. 217.

[9] *The Great Acting Teachers and Their Methods* by Richard Brestoff. Smith and Kraus Books, (1995), p. 53.

[10] *The Great Acting Teachers and Their Methods* by Richard Brestoff. Smith and Kraus Books,(1995), p. 58.

[11] *Strasberg at the Actors Studio* by Robert Hethmon. New York: Viking Press, (1965), p. 78.

[12] *Theatre: A Way of Seeing*, 5th Edition by Milly S. Barranger. Wadsworth Thompson Learning, (2002), pp. 195–6.

[13] Quoted from Strasberg in an interview by Richard Schechner in "Working With Live Material," from the *Tulane Drama Review*, volume 9, #1, Fall, 1964, p. 132.

[14] *The Great Acting Teachers and Their Methods* by Richard Brestoff. Smith and Kraus Books, (1995), p. 114.

[15] *Songs My Mother Taught Me* by Marlon Brando. New York: Random House, (1994), p. 85.

Suggested Exercises

- Select a text with which you will work alone (monologue) or with a partner (scene).
- Create a one-page handout that identifies the objective for your character and lists three potential action verbs that you might use to achieve the objective.
- Schedule a class time to perform your **MEMORIZED** monologue or scene in class.
- You will be evaluated on your written component and the successful completion of your performance component as scheduled.

DESIGNERS AND TECHNICIANS

Rebecca Morrice and Colleen Reilly

CHAPTER OBJECTIVES

- Identify the individuals who design and build for the theatre.
- Describe the responsibilities of the scene designer.
- Describe the responsibilities of the costume designer.
- Describe the responsibilities of the lighting and sound designer.
- Identify the role of the designers in making meaning in the theatre.

Theatrical designers play a vital role in making meaning in the theatre. Designers create the physical reality of a production concept by creating its visual, tactile, and structural elements. Designers create the physical setting of the production and provide the things that are needed to support the action on stage. Designers work closely with the director and each other to co-ordinate the production elements. In some cases this may mean recreating the familiar, and in other cases it may mean inventing things never seen before.

The major areas of theatrical design include scenic design, costume design, lighting design, and sound design. For most productions each of these design components are assigned to a different practitioner. This is due largely to the amount of specialized knowledge needed for each of the design areas. Imagine the different expertise required to build a set or costume, and the differences in lighting and sound technology. A designer not only envisions the design but must have a plan to execute it!

Because of the many areas of expertise required to create the physical world of a theatrical production, there are multiple professional jobs in the areas of theatrical design. The Design and Process Flowchart below describes many of these including the scene designer, technical director, prop master, carpenter, scenic artist, soft goods artisan, props artisan, and props carpenter. This chapter will describe the vital contribution these practitioners make to the overall production process.

KEY TERMS

Carpenter
Cobbler
Costume shop
  manager
Craft master
Cutter/Draper
Designer
Gobo
Ground plan
Milliner
Painter/Dyer
Prop master
Props Artisan
Renderings
'Rough' or 'thumbnail'
  sketches
Scenic artist
Stitcher
Technical director

THE DESIGN AND TECHNICAL PROCESS FLOWCHART

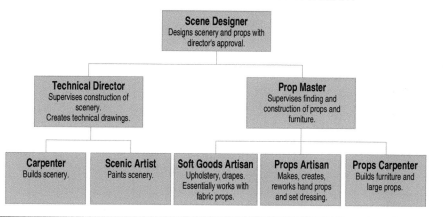

Scene Designers

The *scene designer* is responsible for creating the physical world of the play. Through the design process she must work with the director to materialize the production concept and provide the visual scheme and dimension. Factors that can influence this collaborative process include the style of the production, the orientation of the audience, and any safety considerations.

The style of the production may be the largest determining factor of the scenic design. Scene designers must be well versed in numerous theatrical styles, including historical periods, art history, and historical theatrical productions. You probably noticed that I used the word history several times in that sentence, and for good reason. The first step in much of theatrical design process is research, followed by research, and more research!

The orientation of the audience must also be considered in the design process. Different theatrical spaces (see Chapter Two) have different technical requirements and can require different visual elements. The size and scope of a scenic design is defined by the size and shape of the space in which it will be placed, and a designer must accommodate the movement (or *blocking*) of the actors without interfering with it. In fact, most designers want to create an environment that expands the opportunities for directors and actors to make spatial choices, rather than limit their movement.

One of the most exciting things about the Slippery Rock University Theatre is our ability to use a fixed proscenium space in a variety of seating configurations. Throughout our theatrical season we might use the traditional proscenium, or build thrust, arena, or alley configurations on the Miller Auditorium stage. This allows our student designers and actors the opportunity to experience their craft in a variety of theatrical spaces!

—Colleen Reilly

Safety is an important consideration in the theatre, not only for the actors but the audience as well. The scene designer and technical director communicate throughout the rehearsal process to ensure that design elements meet rigorous safety standards. This can also translate into additional training for the actors in the use of scenic elements. Anything is possible in the theatre, but safety comes first!

The process of communication between the director, scene designer, and **technical director** is supported by the use of *ground plans*, *renderings*, and *models*. These visual tools allow everyone to clearly define the plan and execution of scenic elements. They prevent miscommunication about the design which can cost the production time and resources. They also provide documentation of the production concept that can be useful for other directors, designers, and theatre scholars.

A **ground plan** is a draft of the stage drawn as if looking from above it. It allows designers and directors to communicate about the orientation of the audience as well as the placement of furniture and set pieces. The ground plan is created early in the rehearsal process, so that the director and actors can begin the process of blocking with the design in mind. The ground plan also informs the choices to be made by the lighting designer by showing the playing areas of the actors.

A *rendering* is a draft of the set from the audience's perspective. This allows the designer to communicate the visual elements of his design including the style and use of perspective. The rendering ensures that the concept of the design is aligned with the director's vision, and can also be useful to the costume designer who may choose to incorporate some of the scenic elements (color, line, and texture) in her own design.

A *model* is a three-dimensional representation of the set built to scale. While contemporary designers may create virtual models, it is important for a physical model to exist as well. This allows everyone involved in the process to see and experience how the set will operate before it is completed. The model is particularly helpful in instances when the set only becomes available late in the rehearsal process, because the other practitioners have been prepared for how the set will work in advance.

Costume Designers

The *costume designer* is the artist who is in charge of how a character looks from head to toe. This means that not only is the costume designer working on the clothing, but he also chooses hairstyles, makeup, shoes, hats, and so on. Ultimately the costume designer coordinates the entire look for each character.

The costumes a designer chooses will come from a variety of sources. Some will be found in the theatre's stock of costumes and altered or changed to work, some will be bought, some will be borrowed or rented from other theater companies, and some will be made from new materials.

The most obvious goal I have as a costume designer is to clothe the actor/character. But beyond that, how do I choose the exact items to illustrate each character for the audience?

After reading the play and discussing ideas with the director, I begin by asking one basic question. How much of the characters' personality, background or motivation do I want to reveal to the audience through the costume and how much do I want to conceal? If a character is an evil villain, does the director want the audience to know that right away? In this case, the stereotypical black cape and handlebar moustache might work. Or do we want to fool the audience for a little while and not reveal this fact until later? In that case the cape and moustache would reveal too much. Once I have that answer, I can move on to the next steps of my process.

First, I research the time period the play will be set in. While I have a good understanding of what various time periods looked like, I do not necessarily know exactly what a maid would wear on an English country estate in 1760. While we all have an idea of what the British Redcoats looked like—exactly what were the pieces of clothing they were wearing that created that look? Research is a crucial element in any costume design even if the play is set in a modern era. If I were designing a modern play that had a character who was a part of punk subculture, I would find it quite interesting and exciting to visually research what my options would be to create a believable "punk" onstage. If we were doing a modern play about the war in Afghanistan, it would be very important to me to accurately

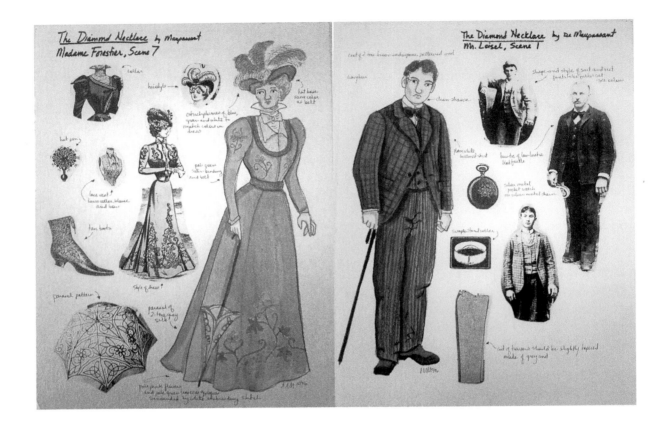

portray onstage the uniforms the soldiers wear today. Even a futuristic or "no-time, no-place" setting will require some research. In order to prepare myself for this kind of design, I will often spend hours looking at the work of some unusual and innovative designers such as Alexander McQueen.

Next, I analyze each character in the play and imagine what would be hanging in their closet if they actually had one. Some of the qualities I may be looking for and deciding whether they should factor in include the following questions.

What is this character's personality?

What is the character's age?

What is the character's social status among the other characters in the play?

How can or should my costumes help the audience to understand when and where this play is taking place?

Can the costumes help the audience to understand the various levels of relationships within the play?

What is this character's occupation?

What are the movement requirements for this character?

What Is This Character's Personality?

Everyone dresses the way they do for a reason. Someone who is a slob will have a very different wardrobe than someone who is a neat freak. Someone who is dark and gloomy will make different choices than someone who is bright and cheery. A costume designer has to be careful with this question because it is easy to do too much through the costume and forget that the actor will also be adding to the director's idea of the character. To be too stereotypical here is an easy mistake and one I am conscious to avoid unless the style of the play calls for it.

What Is the Character's Age?

High school and college theatre departments have a unique challenge on their hands in that many of the actors cast will not be the same age as the characters they are portraying. This results in the need for a lot of extra effort through costume and makeup in order to give the audience the illusion of age. In professional theatre, it is much more likely that a fifty- or sixty-year-old actor will be cast to play a character who is fifty or sixty years old. In educational theater, that is not always possible.

What Is the Character's Gender?

Interestingly enough, this comes up quite often. Not only do directors sometimes like to do what we call gender-bending, which is casting an actor to portray a member of their opposite sex, but there are many plays, both classical and modern, that require a character to portray the opposite sex at points in the play.

Twelfth Night, by William Shakespeare, is a good example of a play in which a female character, Viola, dresses as a man through much of the action of the play and then reveals herself to be a woman at the end. Given that all actors in Shakespeare's day were male, it may also be surprising to note that the original Juliet in Romeo and Juliet was first played by a young man.

What Is the Character's Social Status Among the Other Characters in the Play?

Within any group of characters there will be some who are of a higher social status than others. This may reflect the differences between the rich and poor characters. It may reflect differences in their power status. In any case it is often helpful to at least subtly suggest these differences to the audience.

How Can or Should My Costumes Help the Audience to Understand When and Where This Play Is Taking Place?

The costumes of a play can do a lot to set the play. Clothing looks different in different time periods. Clothing looks different from country to country. Even without a set design, the costumes can aid the audience in understanding whether we are watching a play set in the past, present, or future, and they can aid in understanding where the play is taking place. Football uniforms tell the audience we are at a football game without actually needing the football field. The bustle gown and black top hats help the audience understand that the library the actors are in is from the 1800s rather than a modern time period.

Can the Costumes Help the Audience to Understand the Various Levels of Relationships Within the Play?

This can be a particularly difficult challenge but often become necessary especially with large plays such as Shakespeare's *Romeo and Juliet* where there are two distinct feuding families and a variety of characters who belong to one family or the other. One way to help the audience keep straight who belongs to each is through the use of color. For example, I could choose from the start that anyone related to Juliet will be in shades of blue while anyone from Romeo's family will wear shades of red. This would help the audience to keep straight who belongs to which family whenever they appeared on stage.

What Is This Character's Occupation?

What people do for a living will often greatly affect what they wear. A soldier in any time period will look different than a civilian. A maid will look different than the people living in the house she cleans. A businesswoman will look different than the waitress serving her at a restaurant.

What Are the Movement Requirements for This Character?

If a character will be doing significant movement during the play such as stage combat, dancing, and falls, the costume I design must be able to move with the actor. To ask an actor to sword-fight in clothes that do not allow them to lunge and fall, is asking for a "wardrobe malfunction." There are sewing tricks that can be done to clothing, and fabrics that can be chosen, that will work to accommodate the needs of the movement but you must know this going into the process—not after the actor has split his pants trying to leap across the stage.

These are just some examples of the questions I need to answer before I can begin choosing what each garment is that the characters wear. Very often, the choices are subtle but they must be made for a reason. Remember that everything that you see on stage was chosen to be there. Nothing is arbitrary as we all began with a blank stage and a naked actor.

Color can have a very significant effect on an audience's interpretation of a character. If a character walks out in a long black dress, we might find her elegant. If the same character appeared in the same dress, but in red, we might find her more risqué or daring.

Texture can have a significant impact on our understanding as well. A suit made of rough cotton will hang stiffly and would be more appropriate for a poor character, while the same suit made out of fine silk or wool would give us the impression of someone who can afford to buy his suits from an expensive tailor.

Line can help a character look softer and possibly more feminine if curvilinear, while costumes with a lot of hard, straight lines will appear more austere and masculine.

Now that I have made these decisions, my next job is to put these ideas on paper. I need to illustrate my designs so that a director can see what is in my head and approve or, if necessary, disapprove the look for each character.

First I begin by doing some simple pencil sketches of my ideas on paper. These are called **'rough' or 'thumbnail' sketches** and are usually quick and simple.

Once the director and I are in agreement, I begin the process of creating **renderings** which are color paintings or collages representing the look for each costume within the show.

Details such as hairstyles, shoes, accessories and costume props will also be illustrated at this point because, after they are approved by the director, these renderings will then be passed on to a whole team of people in the costume shop to bring the ideas to life.

While the educational costume shop I am in charge of typically consists of myself, a part-time student assistant, and a few volunteers, professional theatre costume shops are usually made up of many people, each assigned to fulfill a specific set of tasks.

First, there is the **costume shop manager** who is in charge of managing the resources, staff, and workload of the costume shop. This person helps to decide how the costume budget should be spent and is usually quite knowledgeable about where to find items a designer needs—especially when designing for a different time period.

Next there is the *draper* who is an expert dressmaker and tailor. Not only do they have the skills to know how to make a designer's rendering come to life in fabric, they also know how to expertly fit the garments to the actors' specific measurements and they know how to do all of this for clothes from across history. They understand not only how to fit pre-made garments but they also know how to draft patterns for costumes that are to be made from scratch. There are not many people around today who understand the intricacies of an 1880s bustle gown or have a reason to know how to construct a man's Renaissance doublet, so it makes the wealth of knowledge a draper has rather remarkable.

Working closely with the *draper* is the *first hand*, who is often training to become a draper. This is the person who

Costume Designer
Designs costumes, including makeup, hair and, shoes and accessories.

Costume Shop Manager
Supervises construction of costumes. Manages budgets.

Craft Master
In charge of all costume accessories. Jewelry, masks, belts, armor, etc.

Cutter/Draper
Constructs and alters all costumes. Expert Tailor and dressmaker.

Milliner
Hat maker. Costume pieces worn on head.

Painter/Dyer
Paints and dyes fabric. Distresses/ages costumes. Paints shadows.

Cobbler
Shoemaker
Bootmaker

First Hand
Cuts all fabric. Supervises stitchers.

Stitcher
Does all sewing.

takes the draper's pattern and cuts it from the fabric the designer has chosen. While this seems simple enough, the first hand not only knows how to cut the pattern out with all of the proper allowances for the seams, she also knows how to lay it out so that patterns will match up properly and the garment will hang properly. The first hand also supervises the *stitchers*.

The *stitchers* are the team of people who take the garments the draper has marked for alterations or the fabric the first hand has cut out, and finish them. This includes not only sewing the seams of a garment but also all of the finishing work including adding zippers, buttons, decorative trims, and embroidery, and any other part of the process that involves sewing. It is quite common for each draper in a costume shop to have at least one first hand and two or three stitchers assisting them.

While we tend to think of most costumes as fabric, there are many items that an actor may be asked to wear that are not typical pieces of sewn clothing. For instance, armor, shoes, hats, jewelry, and other accessories all fall into

this category. In these cases, the *craftmaster* will create or supervise other artisans in creating these items.

Working alongside the craftmaster will be the *painter/dyer* who is in charge of dyeing any fabric whose color the designer wants to change. As a designer, I don't always have a hard time finding the perfect garment or piece of fabric I want for a costume but it is rarely the exact color I want it to be. In this case, a painter/dyer has the skills and color knowledge to mix the right dyes to change it for me. Additionally, the painter/dyer will also do any distressing or aging of costumes that need to have that look. They will also sometimes paint shadows into the folds of a costume to help combat the bright stage lights that can make scenery and costumes look very flat onstage. They may paint trims, false embroidery, and other special effects onto a costume as well.

Also working with the craft master will be the *cobbler* and the *milliner*. As it is very difficult to find shoes from past time periods, and impossible to afford to purchase the real thing, the cobbler is in charge of making or altering any footwear the designer needs for a performance. Additionally since hats were a common accessory in most time periods all the way up through the 1950s, a theatre will also sometimes employ a milliner who specifically makes hats. If a theatre company specializes in producing works of classical theatre, the jobs of cobbler and milliner can easily be full-time positions.

Wigmakers and *makeup designers* will be employed when a designer needs to significantly alter the style or color of an actor's hair or needs to alter the look of their face or create other makeup special effects. While professional actors, both male and female, are usually trained to be able to do their own basic stage makeup, they are not expected to do their own prosthetics, special effects, or blood effects. As the actors are also not required to dye or cut their own hair, and hairstyles vary greatly from one time period to the next, wigmakers and stylists can very valuable to bring on board.

Finally the *wardrobe crew* is brought in. These are the people who work to maintain, clean, repair, and care for the costumes once the show has opened to audiences. They are also there to help dress the actors when the costumes are complicated or when the actor must perform a quick-change (usually defined as an actor having to change from one costume to another in a very short amount of time, often one minute or less). Depending on the longevity of the run of the play, the wardrobe crew may be employed for days or, in the case of some long-running Broadway performances, for years. Imagine the work it takes to keep the costumes looking as good at their last performance as they did at the first!

As you can see, there is a lot of thought and physical effort put into choosing the clothing the actors will wear as their characters. While many of these choices are meant to be subtle so that they will not be overly obvious to the audience and draw them out of their enjoyment of the performance, the combined effect of these efforts adds to the overall production.

Lighting Designers

Like the scenic and costume designers, the *lighting designer* makes choices that contribute to the realization of the production concept. While lighting design is a fairly recent development in theatrical practice, it is rapidly evolving as lighting technology advances. The lighting designer works very closely with the director and scene designer, and works to create lighting effects that contribute to the mood, atmosphere, and the sensory experience of the audience. Lighting design can also contribute to the audience's understanding of location and time of day.

In creating a lighting design, the lighting designer considers four dimensions of lighting: *intensity*, *color*, *pattern*, and *focus*. The *intensity* of the light is determined by the type of lighting instrument, the strength of its lamp, and the use of any filters. Like all of the lighting dimensions the lighting intensity contributes to the mood, definition of time and place, and dimension of scenic elements. The *color* of the light is determined by the use of lighting gels added to the lighting instruments. A lighting designer uses color to communicate mood and impact the atmosphere of the production. *Pattern* is defined by the type of lamp and the use of special inserts known as **gobos**. Pattern can create shapes on stage, provide texture, and give a sense of place. *Focus* refers to the orientation of the lamps, and is implemented by the lighting designer in the placement and distribution of the lighting instruments. The lighting designer creates a lighting plot to communicate their plan for hanging the lighting instruments.

GOBO

A template for a pattern inserted in a lighting instrument to create a projection or image on the stage.

Sound Designers

Sound design can have a profound impact on the mood or atmosphere of a given moment on stage. It can also provide a sense of time, place, and even memory. Like lighting design, sound design is a rapidly evolving field as technology is developed to support it. Sound designers collaborate with the director to realize a production concept by creating ambient sound, practical sound, and sound that underscores the action of the play.

Ambient sound refers to sound effects that provide information about a particular location. These sound effects are often recorded and might include wind, birds, traffic, office noise, and similar familiar noises. *Practical* sound effects refer to sound design elements that must be created live on stage. A sound design that *underscores* the action of the play resembles a traditional soundtrack, and can create a kind of commentary on the action. A sound designer often has to acquire the rights for tracks included in the underscore.

In addition to creating the sound cues, the sound designer creates a sound plot that describes the placement of microphones, speakers, and other sound auxiliary equipment. This plot must be coordinated with the set designer, lighting designer, and costume designer.

Conclusion

While this chapter has provided an overview of the responsibilities of the scene designer, costume designer, lighting designer, and sound designer, it by no means exhausts the vital role each plays in the process of making theatre. Each designer undergoes a process of research and documentation that not only communicates their vision for the design elements, but also their plan for the execution of that vision. Through drawings, plots, and renderings their unique visions emerge and remain as a record of the production. Designers bridge the gap between the imaginary and the tangible, and translate the creative vision into material reality. That is how they contribute to the making of meaning in the theatre.

Suggested Exercises

- Create a design concept for the scene or monologue selected.
- Create a one-page handout that articulates your design statement.
- **Scenic Design**: Create one of the following:
  o A ground plan and a poster-size collage of magazine clippings or photographs that reflect your scenic design.
  o A color rendering.
  o A shoebox diorama with a multidimensional realization of your design.
- **Costume Design**: Create a poster-size collage of magazine clippings or sketches that reflect your costume design.
- **Sound Design**: Create a ten- to twelve-minute soundtrack for the sound design. Your handout must include the track names and artists.
- Design projects will be displayed for the class. Presentation is optional.
- You will be evaluated on your written component and the timely submission of your design.

PLAYWRIGHTS

David Skeele

CHAPTER OBJECTIVES

- Define action as central to the creation of dramatic text and identify the differences between psychological and physical action.
- Understand the role of the playwright in making meaning in the theatre.
- Discuss different ways that playwrights are inspired to make art.
- Understand the differences between real speech and dramatic text.
- Recognize the importance of creating unique and individualized characters.

KEY TERMS

Eugene O'Neill
Gregory Kotis
Lisa Kron
Moisés Kaufman
Paula Vogel

Of all the artists who come together to create theatre, the playwright occupies a unique position. Directors begin their process with a written script (or, alternately, with a group of actors who are ready to help them create one). Actors and designers also begin with the script, along with any interpretive guidelines or inspiration provided by the director. Stage carpenters and electricians begin with plans provided by the designers. Members of the various backstage crews begin with nearly finished productions.

The playwright, on the other hand, typically begins with nothing. Every play I've ever written has begun life as a sheet of paper or a blank computer screen. How does the playwright deal with this challenge—the challenge of creating art out of thin air?

Playwriting and the Problem of Inspiration

Some playwrights find that their own lives provide rich dramatic material. **Eugene O'Neill**, considered one of the finest playwrights America ever produced, drew heavily on his own family experience to write his Pulitzer Prize-winning 1942 masterpiece *Long Day's Journey Into Night*. The story and characters mirrored those of his own painful upbringing so closely, in fact, that he never submitted the play for production in his lifetime. It was finally staged in 1956—three years after his death. Playwright/performer **Lisa Kron** has fashioned many of her plays, such as *2.5 Minute Ride* and *101 Humiliating Stories*, directly from her own experiences.

There are pitfalls to autobiographical writing, however. Young playwrights (and even experienced playwrights) often find that they have a lack of objectivity about their own lives, making it difficult for them to decide what material to include and what material to discard. Virtually everything in your own life seems meaningful and important to you, but it is not always easy to tell how much of it will translate into a meaningful and important experience for others. For instance, a violent argument you were part of may have been traumatic for you or exciting for you, but will it necessarily prove dramatic when recounted and staged for people who weren't there?

This is one reason most playwrights employ a *partially* or *indirectly* autobiographical approach, perhaps beginning with their own experiences, but transforming the circumstances and the characters enough that they maintain some objectivity about them. (It is worth noting here that NO playwright can completely remove the element of autobiography from his writing. Playwrights are artists, which means that everything they do will be colored by their own unique upbringing and experiences—and that is exactly as it should be!)

Playwright **Paula Vogel** suffered a terrible personal tragedy, losing her brother to AIDS just before they were to embark on a European vacation. Her response was to create the play *The Baltimore Waltz*, but in it she chose not to recount directly the story of his struggle with the disease. Instead, she created a darkly comic vision of what their trip through Europe might have been, in the process changing the terminally ill character from the brother to the sister.

Similarly, **Gregory Kotis**' hit musical *Urinetown* was inspired by an experience he had in Paris, when poor budget planning forced him to spend several days rationing change to use in that city's pay bathrooms. Again, rather than telling the story of a financially strapped playwright trying to survive in Paris, he used his experience to help him create a tale of a dystopian world where all bathrooms are pay bathrooms controlled by a power-mad corporation.

Sometimes playwrights use historical events and/or present-day news stories as inspiration. Sharon Pollock researched the Lizzie Borden murder case of 1893 in order to create her chilling play *Blood Relations*. **Moisés Kaufman** and his Tectonic Theatre Company used another famous murder—the vicious attack on gay college student Matthew Shepard in Laramie, Wyoming—as the backdrop of *The Laramie Project*. In this *documentary play*, playwright Kaufman and his actors interviewed hundreds of Laramie residents, eventually assembling the interview dialogue into an acclaimed three-act play that measures the reverberations of the murder on an entire community.

Upon occasion, playwrights have successfully *combined* the historical event and the present-day news story. In the 1970s, Howard Brenton wrote a play entitled *The Romans In Britain*. Though on its surface it is an historical play about Roman oppression of the native British populace, it is a thinly disguised condemnation of then-current British policies toward Ireland. Probably the most famous example of a playwright using an historical event as an analogy for a contemporary one is Arthur Miller's play *The Crucible*. Though it seems to be an investigation of the famous Salem witch trials of the late seventeenth century, those trials were clearly intended by Miller to be a metaphor for the persecution of American citizens in the 1950s by Senator Joseph McCarthy and the House Committee on Un-American Activities (HUAC).

Some playwrights freely admit to using their own fears and anxieties and anger as inspiration, finding it therapeutic to hold them at arm's length and examine them. As someone who writes plays of supernatural horror, I'm definitely one of those playwrights. My way of beginning one of these plays is to sit in a dark room watching a horror movie or an episode of *Ghost Hunters*, trying to get in touch with the things that truly frighten me.

Many playwrights talk about a play being launched by a single visual image. Such an image might be held in the playwright's mind for months or even years before he understands what it means or realizes how he want to use it. Again, I'll use my own playwriting as an example. For years, I had an image that I simply knew would one day be part of the opening of a play: an image of a young man in a garish heavy-metal t-shirt and a leather vest, wearing an expression at once intense and vacant, sitting next to a throbbing turbine. What did it mean? Who knew? I just felt compelled by this young man and his expression of unfocused rage. When a playwriting professor suggested writing a play for "two guys and a deck of cards," everything came together: I used the image as the basis for *King of Sticks*, a play about a deluded, troubled young man who works in the basement of a paper mill and believes he has the ability to read tarot cards.

Often, plays are simply inspired by ideas for characters: characters who just appear in the playwright's mind's-eye (as in the examples above), characters based on people the playwright observes in real life or people with whom she is acquainted. How many times have you looked at your crazy roommate or eccentric uncle and said "this guy ought to be in a play" (or movie or novel)? Well, if you're a playwright, you're blessed with the ability to actually write that play!

It is fitting that we've come to the subject of character now, for no matter how or where you find inspiration to begin your play, it is character that must be your primary building-block.

Dramatic Characters

Gary Garrison, head of the playwriting program at New York University's Tisch School of the Arts, likes to begin his classes by writing a wonderfully blunt quote on the chalkboard, capitalized for emphasis: "YOUR PLAY WILL NEVER BE MORE DRAMATIC OR INTERESTING THAN THE CHARACTERS YOU PUT IN IT." It's a simple but crucial piece of advice. For many playwrights, it is the *idea* or the *theme* that provides that first spark of excitement. That of course is fine, but far too many beginning playwrights fail to understand that ideas and themes are not in and of themselves dramatic. It is not until the ideas and themes find expression in the mouths of fully realized characters that a play becomes dramatic.

So what is a fully realized character? Think about the characters who have captured your imagination and interest in plays, or in films or television shows or novels. Why did they intrigue you? Certainly it's not a simple matter of being likeable. Some of the most fascinating and memorable characters in dramatic literature have been villains such as Shakespeare's Richard III or Tony Kushner's Roy Cohn. It's been said that great stories are stories that combine the unique and the universal, and the same could be said about great characters: they are unique, different enough from us that we feel we can learn something new from them; and at the same time they are universal, containing recognizable human attributes to which we can all relate.

Of course, building these unique and relatable characters is easier said than done, or everyone would be a successful playwright. How do playwrights do it? They do it the same way anyone who is building anything does: by using tools. And, I would argue, the single most important tool a playwright can bring to bear on the problem of creating memorable characters is empathy. The playwright is an artist who has much in common with the actor. Like the actor, the playwright must find a way to inhabit the character, to get under the skin of the character, to be able to see and hear and feel from the character's perspective. (A notable difference is that while the actor is usually responsible for one character, the playwright must achieve this close connection with all of the play's characters.)

Suppose that a playwright conceives the idea for a play about a woman who realizes that the child upon whom she's lavished attention is a failure as a person, and that the child she's virtually ignored for years has blossomed into someone remarkable. At some point in the play, the woman, Charlene, addresses the disappointing child, Teddy:

> **CHARLENE**
> I can't believe I've lavished all this attention on you, and now you're a lazy slob who can't bring himself to even look for a job, much less move out of my house. Bridget, on the other hand, has really made something of herself. She's a major figure in an important publishing house, making enough money that she's just bought a nice place in the suburbs and an expensive sports car. I've given you everything, made every sacrifice for you, but now I am overcome with guilt and anxiety, and I can't help wondering if it was my influence that made you what you are, and if Bridget became a success *because* I never gave her the time of day.

This, of course, is absolutely wretched writing, and it is wretched for so many reasons that we may be able to come back to it time and time again to find examples of what not to do as a playwright. But the major reason for the wretchedness is that this imaginary playwright has never bothered to put himself in Charlene's shoes. She is not truly a character because he has never really moved past the idea of Charlene. If our playwright had taken the time to truly imagine what Charlene's anguish is like for her, and to fully explore the ambiguous feelings she has for her children, her monologue might have sounded like genuine human speech. Because Charlene remains an idea, however, her words sound far more like a passage lifted from a textbook.

The playwright must know not only what a character expresses, but also how the particular character expresses it, which brings us to another important playwriting tool: an ear for dialogue.

Dramatic Dialogue

There is a misconception, shared by a surprising number of people, that the objective of playwriting is to create dialogue that closely mimics the way people talk in real life. A playwright, according to this theory, is essentially a human tape recorder, whose job it is to transcribe the genuine conversation of the street onto the stage. However, all it takes to utterly disprove this notion is the use of an actual tape recorder. Record a conversation between people and you may indeed occasionally hear a fascinating word choice, or sometimes pick up on the musicality of a well-turned phrase. But these nuggets of worthwhile dialogue will be buried under a mountain of stammering, of repetition, of throwaway lines and meaningless words. In short, normal conversation, like commercial breakfast cereal, is ninety-five percent filler. The playwright's job is not to transcribe but to carefully weed out the filler, and then to shape and mold and craft until they have boiled down the ordinary into its marvelous essence. This final product will bear the same resemblance to ordinary speech that a finely wrought metal sculpture bears to lumps of iron ore buried in a hillside.

The comparison between the playwright and the sculptor is a useful one, but perhaps the stone or wood sculptor makes for an even more apt analogy, since paring away words is as big a part of the playwright's job as creating them.

For an example, let's return to Charlene's speech above. We've agreed (I hope) that it sounds woodenly, painfully unrealistic—more like an essay than a person. I'll argue that one of the reasons for this is that, like the writer of a bad textbook, Charlene uses too many words. She baldly states things when a mere hint would suffice. She tediously explains points that we presumably already understand. She describes emotional states that should be readily apparent to everyone watching her. All of this overwriting has the effect of making us feel that the playwright is talking down to us—that he or she thinks that we are too stupid to figure anything out for ourselves.

So how do we boil this speech down to its essence? What do we chip out to reveal the life hidden within it? One of the oldest pieces of advice given to playwrights (and screenwriters and fiction writers) is "show, don't tell." What does this mean? Essentially it means that audiences (and readers) would much rather decipher truths about the characters by witnessing their behavior, rather than by simply trusting their words. If you were, say, at a party, which of these people would you find more convincing: someone who walks up to you and announces "I'm very charismatic," or someone who enters a room with a confidence and energy that draws the attention of everyone there?

Rather than having Charlene announce the facts about Teddy (which have probably been at least somewhat established by this point in the play), why not show us Teddy's flaws in action? And why have Charlene state that she is "overcome with guilt and anxiety?" Can't we see that in everything she says and does? Is all the specific information about Bridget really necessary? Taking all of these questions into account, let's go Michelangelo on this stupid monologue and see if we can't improve it.

(*Lights up on Teddy, sitting on a couch with a television remote in his hand. He stares blankly at an invisible television screen, every once in while lazily thumbing the channel button. Charlene enters. She stays in the doorway watching him for a few moments, anguish in her features. Though he registers her presence, he doesn't acknowledge her. After an internal struggle, she speaks.*)

CHARLENE
Any calls?

TEDDY
Uh-uh.

Continued

CHARLENE
I thought there might be news from one of the…you know…job interviews.

TEDDY
There wasn't.
(He continues to flip channels, not looking at her.)

CHARLENE
Bridget called. She bought a house. In *Sewickley.*
(Perhaps Teddy grunts something noncommittal.)
And she did it all by herself. No help from me. Never any help from me. I mean…isn't that *nice?* To be able to buy a house? To just have the money to…to…
(Teddy flips another channel. In a sudden rage, Charlene rips the remote from his hand and smashes it on the floor. Teddy stares dumbly at her.)
I've given you everything, everything I could. Guided you. Held your little hand every step of your life and…look at you! Just look at you!
(Pause. A bitter realization.)
It's me, isn't it? It must be. What if I'd just left you alone? Ignored you. The way I did with…Bridget.
(In tears, she runs from the room, leaving Teddy gaping after her.)

Okay, there's still nothing here to make me devoutly wish this play really existed, but most would agree that this piece is a lot more dramatic and interesting than the original. And I have to admit that I did more than merely cut away a lot of Charlene's words—I added in a number of stage directions and threw in the character of Teddy while I was at it. The "addition by subtraction," however, is in my opinion one of the most significant improvements, since it allows you as the audience member or reader the fun of filling in some of the blanks yourself.

Notice, too, that Charlene no longer speaks in formal, neutral, "textbook" sentences. Her speech is timid, halting, full of ellipses (the …s), and so we know immediately that she is unsure of herself and nervous about confronting her spoiled son. Teddy's manner of speaking tells us something about him, too—namely that he is so lazy that he uses the absolute minimum number of words necessary to communicate.

Action—The Lifeblood of a Play

You may have noticed one other thing that makes the second version of our hypothetical scene more satisfying: it contains *action*. In the first, Charlene is simply

We talked about objective and actions in the previous chapter: this is what drives the character to get what he wants: he does this by pursuing actions. What do you do to get what you want? What tactics to you play? What does Charlene want from Teddy? Let's keep it simple: she wants him to get a job. How does she try to make that point in the scene? She hints, she cajoles, she paints the picture of her daughter's success, she explodes, she plays the martyr.

—Laura Smiley

reciting a list of facts, which is about as interesting for an audience as watching kumquats ripen. In the second, however, she is actually doing something.

We witness her trying to summon up the nerve to confront her son, first trying to prod his conscience with gentle hints, and then finally erupting and proceeding to berate him. Even the dumbstruck Teddy has a modicum of action, in that he's struggling to get his mind around the shocking things his mother is saying to him. Do you see the difference?

Action is really what we come to the theatre to see. Even more than brilliant dialogue or beautiful costumes or dazzling stage effects, it's the promise of action that lures us out of the comfort and convenience of home, that convinces us to sacrifice our hard-earned money and leisure time. It may not be the action of film, with its realistic car chases and helicopter explosions—it is usually psychological action—but nevertheless, if a play contains strong dramatic action it will probably be riveting, and if it does not it certain to be deadly dull. We want to see people who need things, and then we want to see them fighting for those things. We want to see them scratching and clawing and seducing and praying and lying and fearing and daring and resisting and submitting. In short, we want to see verbs, lots of verbs, and at the end of the day it is the playwright's job to give them to us. (Directors and actors spend countless hours trying to find the most exciting verbs to play in each scene, but all of their efforts will be in vain if the playwright hasn't given them exciting action to begin with!)

Again, some young playwrights may be misled into static, passive writing by following the misguided notion that theatre is a "reflection of life." Life, like bad dialogue, contains a lot of filler—long stretches of inactivity, of tedium and monotony. But theatre is not really a reflection of life. It is instead, as Alfred Hitchcock famously said, "life without the boring parts."

Writers are often told to "write what they know," so many beginning playwrights try to dramatize safe, familiar situations from their own lives. Being a teacher of college-age students, I can't tell you how many idle dorm-room conversations I've had presented to me as plays. But these conversations, featuring no strong character need (beyond the desire to gossip about what girl or guy is the hottest) or action (beyond mere chattering), are usually not even slightly dramatic, and so no matter how amusing they might seem, they would paralyze an audience with boredom if they were ever produced.

Successful, dramatic, active plays feature characters faced with some kind of crisis, a crisis that requires the characters to do something: to defeat an adversary, to acquire money or position, to convince the crotchety parents to let him marry their daughter, etc., etc. In *Hamlet*, the title character is thrown into crisis when the ghost of his father appears and demands that he avenge his murder. In *A Streetcar Named Desire*, the fading Southern belle Blanche Dubois is thrown into crisis when scandal (and miserable financial straits) forces her to take refuge in a tenement apartment with her sister and brutal, loudmouthed brother-in-law. In both cases, the character has no choice but to take action to try and rectify the situation, and in both cases the odds are sharply stacked against them.

This last point is crucial, because the more difficult the objective for the character, the greater the conflict, and thus the greater the dramatic tension. Blanche is so emotionally fragile, and she is so disliked by the boorish Stanley Kowalski, that it takes everything she has just to survive, and that's exactly what makes watching her so compelling. If Blanche had immediately adapted to her new surroundings and made fast friends with Stanley not only would there be no tension, there would be no play. Similarly, if our hypothetical play is to be any good, Charlene will face serious conflict. Teddy won't immediately run after his mother, vowing to become a company CEO by sundown. instead he'll engage in some crafty passive-aggressive strategy to continue getting her financial support. Bridget won't immediately become her mother's best friend. she'll be antagonistic, and force Charlene to try to break through walls forged of years of resentment.

If we can define a play as a character's struggle, we could just as accurately define it as a character's journey, and like any journey, it must end somewhere different than it begins. Charlene seems to have begun this play as a well-meaning person who is also a woefully blind and misguided mother, doting on her son and disconnected from her daughter. She is also fearful and non-confrontational. What lies at the end of her journey? Maybe she grows as a result of her terrible mistake: she finally establishes the relationship she always should have had with her daughter, and finds the strength to force her needy, manipulative son out of the nest and into the world. Or maybe she is brutally rejected by Bridget and tries to come back to Teddy, who now rejects her too, until she ends the play as a suicidal alcoholic. Who knows? The point is that Charlene and her world must change. It may be the promise of action that draws the audience member into their theatre seat—but it's the promise of transformation that keeps them there until the lights come down.

Setting

While we've radically improved our play by empathizing with the character, listening to how she might actually talk, and adding the element of action to her situation, there is one element that remains kind of unexciting: the setting. In creating this scene, I did what I constantly caution my students not to do—I just threw my characters into a standard living room. Living rooms, like bus stops, park benches and the infamous dorm room, are what we call a "default setting," a place where playwrights stash their characters just to save themselves the trouble of imagining anything more unusual.

Can effective plays be set in these places? Of course. Edward Albee wrote a brilliant park bench play called *Zoo Story*. William Inge's *Bus Stop* couldn't possibly be set anywhere else. The living room is the heart of the American family home (many would argue for the kitchen), so naturally many family dramas are going to take place there. But I ask my student playwrights to challenge themselves with this question: are any of these settings really the most interesting you can find for your play, or are they just the first you thought of?

I suppose I put Charlene and Teddy in a living room so that Teddy could be watching television. I considered mindless channel-surfing to be the ultimate emblem of laziness, but it's possible that that assumption is also a kind of default. If I had set the piece instead at, say, the Boston Aquarium, it would have opened up all kinds of new possibilities. Perhaps instead of channel-surfing, Teddy spends each day sitting and watching fish. Why? I have no idea, but I could have a lot of fun finding out, and already a fish-watching Teddy seems far more intriguing than a monosyllabic couch potato. He's a character with secrets and issues of his own. The Boston setting requires a colorful accent and vibrant rhythms and (for me) unusual word choices. Research about the area, and perhaps about the varieties of marine life found in an aquarium, would most likely be required (and research is a good thing—it gives you all kinds of new ideas to use!). Finally, putting them in an aquarium means that Charlene didn't just happen upon Teddy—she had to put on a coat, get into a taxi and cross town to talk to him, and that raises the stakes of the confrontation for both of them. See? All of these wonderful new possibilities, and all we had to do was get them out of their generic living room.

It wouldn't have taken such a major shift in setting to change the play. Simply changing the time to 3:30 in the morning or imagining the blizzard of the decade howling outside would have also opened up new options for the playwright. The important thing is that the playwright be specific about these things. The same way playwrights must learn to live and breathe their characters, they must learn to fully imagine their settings. If the setting is chosen well and imagined fully, then it almost becomes another character in the play, influencing the action and affecting all of the other characters. (As someone who writes plays about haunted houses, I am perhaps especially attuned to this idea!)

A Final Word

As this discussion of playwriting basics comes to a close, let's return for a moment to the question of inspiration. I've intentionally left out, until now, the thing that might serve as the best inspiration for writing: writing itself. If you think you'd like to try writing a play, don't think for a moment that you need to have the entire thing conceived from lights up to lights down. All you need is the briefest opening: a bit of dialogue, an image, a character. Write that, and I can practically guarantee you that as you are writing that another line will occur to you, and then another image, and maybe a new character will enter and you can hear exactly what they're saying as they enter. Before you know it you'll have a scene, and by the time you've finished that scene you'll have an idea for the next one, and by the time you finish...you get the idea. The point is: write!

Conclusion

The task of the playwright is to create art out of thin air. Beginning with a blank page, the playwright uses setting, action, and character to create the script that guides the directors, actors, and designers towards production. While the playwright is often an invisible collaborator, they are central to the process of making meaning in the theatre.

Suggested Exercises

Writing from a Premise

Sometimes it is easier to conceive of a story when you have a sense of what you want to "prove."

Following is a list of well-known proverbs. Choose one that you find especially interesting or provocative and jot down a brief summary of a story that might demonstrate the truth of the proverb. (Alternately, you might have fun creating a story that demonstrates the *un*truth of the proverb!)

- A little knowledge is a dangerous thing.
- A friend to all is a friend to none.
- A man's got to do what a man's got to do.
- A rolling stone gathers no moss.
- Act in haste, repent at leisure.
- Actions speak louder than words.
- Any port in a storm.
- Ashes of love are cold as ice.
- Bend like a willow or break like an oak.

Creating Interesting Dialogue

One of the biggest mistakes young playwrights often make is creating characters who all sound the same.

As a playwright, you have a nearly infinite variety of verbal expression to draw from! Don't settle for cliché or characters who sound like they're reading from textbooks.

The following are a list of "dialogue attributes." Pick two that sound interesting to you (make sure they differ from *each other*!), and use them to create a short dialogue between two characters.

Don't worry about plot for now. Just have fun letting two people with wildly different communication methods talk to each other!

12 Dialogue Attributes:
1. Gruff; economical with words.
2. Sinuous; smooth; snake-like with words.
3. Uneducated, and overcompensating through use of words.
4. Barely able to find the breath to convey all the words in his or her head.
5. Lyrical; a poet.
6. Always groping for words; rarely finding them.
7. Everything expressed in a nervous laugh.
8. Sensualist; chews and savors words.
9. Speaks words as though she or he hates the taste of them.
10. Uses sounds of words to seduce.
11. Uses sounds of words to hurt or seize power.
12. Very educated; tries to hide it through use of words.

Character Objectives

Remember, drama is driven by the needs of the characters. Write a short play using the following template:

Two characters, **A** and **B**, who know each other.

Setting is someplace interesting.

A is in crisis, and comes to **B** with a desperate need. **B** is shocked by the need. **A** makes several attempts to get **B** to go along with him/her, but **B** resists. Finally, **B** reveals his/her own need, which shocks **A** even more. At the end, the relationship is either strengthened or shattered or in some way seriously altered.

Suggested Exercises: Practitioners and Process

Playwright Script Assignment

In addition to these instructions, your instructor can provide examples that will aid you in putting your project in the proper format.

> READ ALL INSTRUCTIONS FIRST AND THEN COMPLETE THESE STEPS IN ORDER.

1.) **Read This BLANK SCRIPT.**

A: I thought you'd never get here.

B: Well, I'm here.

A: Obviously. Are you staying?

B: What do you think?

A: I wouldn't know. You're such a mystery.

B: You talk too much.

A: I'm leaving.

B: Where are you going?

A: Not far. Don't get excited.

B: When?

A: Now.

2) **Develop your script SCENARIO or PLOT.**

A) There doesn't seem to be much of anything happening in this scene as it is because it lacks important details. Begin your project by inventing two characters whose interaction in this scene would make it interesting for an audience to watch. It is important that these two characters be your own <u>original</u> creations. Don't use characters that already exist (e.g., famous people, historical characters, comic book heroes) because it limits your creativity in inventing characters and scenarios.

- **WHO?** <u>Write two paragraphs</u>, with each one describing in detail one of your characters. You should include their name, age, physical description, and <u>most importantly</u>, their personality and background. The personality information especially helps an actor to form his or her character. Remember that a script is basically like a set of instructions you hand to an actor, so your details must be complete enough to get your intentions across, but open enough to leave room for the actors to add their own interpretations. If you want to, you can also include photos or drawings of your characters if they help to explain your ideas.

B) Now, imagine a scenario and location where your two characters might come together to say the lines above. Often playwrights have strong characters in their minds but need to "let them loose" into a location or situation to "see what happens."

- **WHAT and WHY?** <u>Write one paragraph</u> explaining <u>what</u> is happening in the scenario you are inventing and <u>why</u> it is happening. It is clear that these two people have met or at least spoken before because they have made arrangements to meet each other. Include information about how they know each other, why they are meeting, and what has happened to make this scene take place. Why is the one character late?

  HINT: It is best not to choose a scene such as a boyfriend and girlfriend meeting in a coffee shop arguing about why one of them is yet again late. This kind of scene is too commonplace, and an audience will have a difficult time caring/*empathizing* about what is happening. Be sure that the scenario you pick makes what is happening <u>very important</u> (*dramatic weight*) to at least one of the characters so that the audience will care to know what comes next (*suspense*). Your characters need to be trying to achieve something in this scene (*objective*), and the consequences (*stakes*) if they don't achieve their objective should be high enough that the *dramatic tension* is clear to the audience/reader.

- **WHERE?** <u>Write one paragraph</u> detailing <u>where</u> this scene is taking place. If it is a bar, is it a swanky martini bar, a loud sports bar, a seedy whiskey bar? Details become important here: What is the lighting like? Are other people around? What are the other sounds?

- **WHEN?** <u>Write one paragraph</u> detailing <u>when</u> this scene is taking place. *When* means everything from time of day, season of the year, to the year itself. You could have this scene take place in the past, present, or future; make your choice to create an interesting scene with real *dramatic weight*.

C) Now, write additional lines to the script to make it your own and to make the given dialogue work even better with your invented scenario.

- **ADD** at least 30 lines of dialogue to your script. <u>**Do not change or delete any of the lines that were given**</u> as they are the basis for your scripts. These lines can be added to the beginning, the end, and throughout the scene in general. Add lines where it helps to make your chosen scenario clearer.

- In these 30 lines, a portion of them should be used to create a *monologue* for one of the characters. A *monologue* is "a part of a play in which one character speaks alone; soliloquy. A monologue is a piece of oral or written literature (i.e. a story, poem or part of a play) spoken by one person who exposes inner thoughts and provides insights into his or her character." From *Fundamentals of Acting Glossary*, http://vtheatre.net/acting/dict.html

D) FORMAT

- Change A and B to be the names of your characters.

- Give your play a **title**. The usual convention is that a play title is either underlined, italicized, boldfaced or a combination of the three; that is, **The Crucible**, *The Crucible*, or ***The Crucible***.

- **Boldface** all spoken lines. *Italicize* all unspoken information and stage directions.

- Single-space your entire script, except add one extra line space to separate each character's lines from the next.

Director Script Assignment

In addition to these instructions, your instructor can provide examples that will aid you in putting your project in the proper format.

Using your finished Playwright Script Assignment, complete the following additional steps.

Director Assignment

1) After your script is written, it is time to put your director's cap on and try to imagine how you would have your actors move and speak during each line of your play. *Blocking* is the term used to refer to any of the actors' major movements onstage (how they enter, how they walk, when they sit down), whereas *business* refers to any of the small-scale things they do that help round out their character and possibly reveal personality details to the audience (e.g., nervous fidgeting, chewing gum, foot tapping, gestures, facial expressions). As a director, it is important to let your actors invent some of these things themselves, but for this assignment you will be detailing the most important parts of this.

A *stage direction* in a script can be a physical description of a character, a description of an emotional state a character is in, or a movement, blocking, or other business performed by the actor.

Stage directions are usually in parentheses and *italicized*. (*Stage directions should look like this.*)
Stage directions that describe <u>how</u> an actor says a line should be placed <u>before</u> the spoken line.
Stage directions that describe an <u>action</u> should be placed exactly where the action happens.

<u>**Add a minimum of 15 stage directions**</u> to your script to help your actors/ readers understand your intentions. Remember that stage directions can describe the mood someone is in, <u>how</u> they say a certain line, or describe important actions of the character. See EXAMPLES provided by the instructor for ideas.

HINT: The very first stage direction should deal with how and when Character B enters for the first time. It should also deal with what Character A is doing until Character B arrives (again, see EXAMPLES provided by your instructor).

Design Script Assignment

Using your finished Playwright/Director Script Assignments, complete the following additional steps.

PROJECT SYNOPSIS: You will be designing the set and costumes for your play by doing the following:

- Carefully choose what your characters will be wearing (costume) and what the environment (set) looks like that the scene takes place in.
- Describe your design choices in writing.
- Create COLOR drawings (if you can draw) or COLOR collages (if you are less comfortable drawing) based on the instructions below.
  a.) Collage 1/Drawing 1: Character 1 Costume Design
  b.) Collage 2/Drawing 2: Character 2 Costume Design
  c.) Collage 3/Drawing 3: The Set Design
- Neatly present and label your project.

What is a Collage?

A collage is a collection of items, arranged and attached to a piece of paper. Collages for this project can include magazine photos, photographs, swatches of fabric, hand drawings, color chips or paint chips, or paint, among other things. Collages can be created by cutting and pasting the above items to a piece of paper (preferably 8-1/2 × 11), or by creating it with word-processing software (such as Microsoft Word or Publisher) on the computer by cutting and pasting images into a single document. They can also be a combination of computer and cut-and-paste projects. Choose whichever method best serves your design and abilities. For examples, see http://www.texasbeyondhistory.net/waxcamps/images/maincollage.jpg OR

http://www.polyvore.com/cgi/set?id=75458 OR
http://shannonschweitzer.com/collage2.jpg OR
http://lh3.ggpht.com/jessicacwaks/SDWPi_sSNHI/AAAAAAAADbY/bVkyZp3F5uk/image_thumb%5B43%5D.png.

Costumes

- Create a costume design for <u>each</u> of your characters. A costume includes ANYTHING that has to do with how a character looks—clothing, makeup, hairstyle, shoes, jewelry, tattoos, etc.
  - Visit a website such as www.costumes.org (see the history section) for research if your play is set in a previous time period or just to get ideas for your costumes.
  - Describe in a written paragraph for <u>each</u> character the characters' style, time period, colors, accessories, and so on, <u>and WHY</u> you made those particular choices.

- Create a color drawing or color collage for <u>each</u> character. You may also combine the techniques to illustrate your choices. Do not forget to include hairstyles, accessories, and so forth for each of your characters.
  - If you are comfortable drawing and can express your ideas adequately in this format, you may create COLOR DRAWINGS.
  - Alternatively, most students choose to cut and paste pictures found online to a word-processing document; in that case, you should choose the COLOR COLLAGES. See the example Web links above.
- Clearly label each collage with the name of the play, your name, and the name of the character.

Set

- Create a set design for your scene or monologue. A set includes ANYTHING that has to do with the physical environment in which an actor performs— floors, walls, furniture, backgrounds, props, etc.
  - Describe in a written paragraph the mood of the environment, style, time period, colors, floor treatments, props, set decoration, and so forth, <u>and WHY</u> you made those particular choices.
  - Create a drawing, collage, or combination of the two to illustrate your choices. You should detail important colors, furniture, props, or backgrounds and anything that helps to convey the overall feel or atmosphere of the set. Don't forget to think about the angle from which the audience will view your set.
  - Clearly label your collage with the name of the play and your name.
- **GRADING:** Your grade will be based on:
  - COLLAGES: Are your collages complete and your ideas clear? Are all the elements required present in your collage? Design Choices: Do choices support the script? Do they aid in understanding the play?
  - WRITTEN PARAGRAPHS: Are explanation notes included to explain your choices? Did you explain WHAT you chose and WHY?
  - PRESENTATION: Is the project neatly/professionally presented and labeled?

All assignments that meet the above criteria will receive full credit. Any assignments that do not follow the above guidelines will receive only partial credit.

PRODUCERS

Colleen Reilly

CHAPTER OBJECTIVES

- Understand the role of producers in making meaning in the theatre.
- Understand the responsibilities of the producer in the commercial theatre.
- Identify the process of producing commercial theatre.
- Understand the responsibilities of the managing director in the nonprofit theatre.
- Understand the challenges of producing theatre in the current economic climate.

KEY TERMS

Cost disease
Dramaturg
Property
Run
Royalty pool

I think the best place to start a discussion of producers is with the Broadway musical of the same name. *The Producers*, a musical written by Mel Brooks and Thomas Meehan, opened on Broadway in 2001 and tells the story of a down-on-his-luck Broadway producer who schemes to make a profit by staging the worst musical ever. Set in New York in 1957, the premise of the musical rests on the idea that if a surplus of money is raised to invest in a production that no one has any interest in salvaging, the producers can pocket the money for personal gain. They choose a property called *Springtime for Hitler*, and hire an incompetent director along with an unknown lead actress. Unfortunately, the intent of staging a ridiculous production backfires and they find themselves with a hit on their hands.

The musical raises some interesting questions about the strange economy of producing commercial theatre, and the ethics of the person responsible for the financial matters surrounding the production. Max Bialystock, the fictional producer in *The Producers* is based on a romanticized notion of commercial production from the heyday of Broadway in the 1950s. This chapter will explore the reality of producing theatre in our current economic climate.

Some critics see Max Bialystock as a comic representation of Broadway producer David Merrick. David Merrick was an award winning producer on Broadway from 1954 through 1996. He was a prolific producer responsible for productions like *Oliver!*, *Hello, Dolly!*, and *42nd Street*. He was (in)famous for his publicity stunts which included finding New Yorkers who shared the names of leading theatre critics, soliciting their approval of particular productions, and publishing the statements in the press. In 1998 he established the David Merrick Arts Foundation to support the development of American musicals. When his obituary appeared in the *New York Times* in 2000 it read, "The Showman who Ruled Broadway."

Responsibilities of the Producer

In commercial theatre the role of the producer is a clearly defined, professional-ized position. The producer must complete a sequence of tasks from scouting the **property**, to arranging auditions, rehearsals, and performances, to managing the production during its **run**.

PROPERTY

In theatrical terms, the full scale production including the book (or play), design, directorial choices, blocking and acting choices. The term *property* allows a producer to treat the dynamic creative processes contributing to a theatri-cal creation as a single financed outcome; the product of the collaborative rehearsal process in theatre becomes a single property for the producer that can define the distribution of revenue and expenses.

RUN

The sequence of performances of a single theatrical property. In the commercial sector the *run* of the show is determined by its financial viability. In the nonprofit sector, the run of the show is normally predetermined by the season schedule in a fixed term.

The producer serves the financial interests of the production, but this does not necessarily mean that he is out of touch with the artistic goals of the production staff. A successful producer possesses the same passion for theatrical practice as other practitioners such as the director, actors, and designers; however, the producer has the additional responsibility of translating that vision into a marketable commodity. The expertise and creativity that a producer brings to the process of making meaning in the theatre is not only the ability to reach an audience, but also the ability to maximize the income of a property while minimizing its expenses.

The first step in the producing process is to find and develop a property. In the commercial sector this often occurs as a result of pursuing contacts in literary management and capitalizing on a strong network of theatre contacts. In other words, it boils down to a "who you know" context. This is not to say that commercial producing is always driven by celebrity or wealth; often the "who you know" is determined by serious academic programs like the repertory theatres developed by universities such as Harvard, Yale, and Northwestern. These strong academic programs develop playwrights and practitioners who need an opportu-nity to embrace the commercial theatre. The contemporary American producer often creates a bridge between regional dramaturgs and professional companies for these up and coming voices.

DRAMATURG

A professional position in a theatre company that deals primarily with the development of plays. Dramaturgs support the creation of new plays, contemporary treatments of classic plays, and historical interpretations of plays. In the United States the title dramaturg is interchangeable with literary manager.

Once the property has been determined, the producer must obtain the rights for the production. This is often a complicated process and requires a savvy knowledge of intellectual property and copyright laws. For a classic or historical play, the producer must determine the eligibility of the text for public domain. For more recent plays, the producer must negotiate with the estate of the playwright. For new works, the producer must negotiate a contract with the playwright themselves. Acquiring the rights for production is often the largest obstacle to producing a play or musical; often the rights are simply too expensive to create a viable property.

Consider this: If the capacity of a theatre is 300 seats and the price of student admission is set at $5, this yields a maximum of $1,500 for a full house of student admissions. Therefore, any rights negotiated for a production in this space must cost less than $1,500 per performance in order to begin to generate an income for the production and support future projects. In general, considerations are given for the capacity of the theatre and its commercial or nonprofit status; however, you can see where the tension between the cost of rights to a play and the ability to make a profit starts!

Once the rights have been acquired the commercial producer must legally form the property. This usually occurs as the creation of an **LLC**, or limited liability corporation. An LLC allows multiple investors to create a corporate entity while protecting their overall assets. The executors of an LLC are only responsible for their initial investment, and in the event that the property fails, the rest of their assets remain safe.

In 2010 an LLC was formed with the intention of creating a revival of the musical *Godspell* for Broadway. The interesting approach of this LLC was that it was subject to crowd funding. Investments were divided into $100 units, with a minimum investment of $1,000. This allowed anyone with an interest in producing on Broadway and/or fans of the musical (and $1,000 in disposable income) the opportunity to participate in a situation that had otherwise been closed to them.

When the corporate producing entity is in place the producer next has the responsibility of raising the money for production of the property. This generally involves enlisting other investors to join the LLC, but sometimes leads to finding corporate sponsors as well. Broadway musicals generally require between $10 and $20 million in capital to produce. Broadway plays average about $2 million in capital. The capital is the target amount to be raised to bring a property from its inception to opening night.

Once the money has been raised and significant interest in the property has been expressed, the producer must secure the theatre in which the production will have its run. This decision is determined by the physical theatre's capacity, location, and availability. Producers often create longstanding relationships with Broadway theatres in order to create the leverage that they need to secure the space for the property. As discussed in Chapter Three, the number of Broadway theatres is limited by geographical location and capacity, making the securing of a commercial space a highly competitive task.

The producer also secures contracts with the artistic and production staff through negotiations with professional organizations and unions. Part of the contract negotiations is determining the **royalty pool**, or percentage of receipts that the major practitioners should share. The royalty-pool system is based on the idea that the major parties invested in the property—producers, director, author, and theatre—should recoup some income any week that the production runs. It is an alternative to the system that allows payment to these entities and individuals only after the initial investors have been repaid. The royalty pool allows the major contributors to any property to receive consistent income.

While the creative team develops the property in rehearsal, the producer supervises the marketing campaign and ticket revenues. Finally, the producer manages the production after its opens including monitoring budgets and merchandising, and managing personnel. In return the commercial producer generally receives two percent of the gross receipts. For a Broadway play this can mean as little as $5,000 per week and in some cases as much as $335,000 per week for a Broadway musical.

Responsibilities of a Managing Director

In the nonprofit sector, the managing director of a theatre often takes on the responsibilities of the producer. In this scenario the primary difference between a producer and a managing director is that the producer is working towards their own personal gain, and the managing director is supporting the mission of the nonprofit organization. This means that the revenue generated by a property in the nonprofit sector must be reallocated to the activities of the organization. Both the producer and the managing director share profit as their primary goal, but the distribution of that income is very different.

Like the commercial producer, the managing director of a nonprofit theatre develops properties, acquires the rights, negotiates contracts, and raises capital. However, a managing director operates within a strategic plan or long term vision for a theatre organization. Rather than working independently, a managing director collaborates with other leadership in the nonprofit organization like the artistic director or the Board of Directors.

Nonprofit organizations are not one size fits all, and the structure of the organization's leadership is often determined by the mission of the organization. For example, an organization with a strong educational mission might operate with an artistic director and director of education, and they might share responsibilities that would otherwise fall under the title of the managing director. The bottom line is that in creating a theatrical production someone has to be responsible for coordinating the spaces, the practitioners, and the action.

Unlike the commercial producer, the managing director does not think in terms of the run of the show, but the season of the nonprofit theatre. The number of performances of a particular production are predetermined by the theatre's season. For instance, the Slippery Rock University Theatre plans on four mainstage plays in its season, two in the spring and two in the fall. Like many other educational and nonprofit theatres, we share our space with numerous organizations such as the Dance and Music Department, the Performing Arts Series, and the Kaleidoscope Arts Festival. This means that even if a production is successful and there is a demand for more tickets to additional performances, we must close the production because of other scheduled events. Many nonprofit organizations find themselves in this position, and part of the responsibility of the managing director is to maximize the profit potential in the time available within the season.

Challenges of Producing Theatre

One of the major challenges facing all theatrical producing is the harsh reality of **cost disease**. Professional salaries determined by union negotiations continue to reflect the rising cost of living (and they should!). As they increase so do production expenses such as theatre rent and utilities, building materials for scenery and costumes, and equipment. Marketing costs such as advertising, programs, and promotional materials have also increased significantly in recent years.

COST DISEASE

A rise in labor costs without an increase in productivity. Originally studied for the performing arts sector by William J. Baumol and William G. Bowen. They observed that the same number of musicians are required to play a piece of classical music today as when it was composed in previous centuries, but the cost of compensating the musicians continues to increase.

Ticket sales generate substantial revenue for both commercial and nonprofit theatres. For nonprofits, the revenue from ticket sales provides evidence that the organization is meeting their mission and serving the public. In the commercial sector ticket sales indicate the demand for the property. However, all ticket sales are limited to the capacity of the theatre and the number of times that a production can be staged. Furthermore, the performing arts have the additional challenge of fixed costs in that the number of practitioners required for any production is largely predetermined. For example, the cast of the musical *Cats* must always include the number of characters that Andrew Lloyd Webber composed. A modest production of Shakespeare's *A Midsummer Night's Dream* still must include lovers, fairies, and mechanicals. While reducing the number of actors is often an artistic strategy, it is rarely a financial one.

In order to address the cost disease, producers and managing directors find strategies to raise revenue in other areas. Producers often turn to corporate sponsorship. Broadway theatre properties are particularly attractive to major sponsors. Managing directors increase revenue by securing grants and seeking donors from the public and private sectors.

Conclusion

Producing theatre is a challenging process in both the commercial and nonprofit sector. A producer must have a complete understanding of the value of theatre in terms of both its artistic and economic value. The process of creating a property, arranging for rehearsals and performances, supervising the marketing and sales, and managing the run can take a tremendous investment of time, money, and resources. However, producers reap the financial rewards as well as the satisfaction of bringing great art into the world. Managing directors secure the longevity of their nonprofit organizations and ensure that their practitioners will continue to have a place to perform. Producers make meaning in the theatre by creating the opportunities for theatre to happen in a challenging economic environment.

Suggested Exercises: Producer Project

Name of your Theatre Company

For this project, you will be creating a plan for a new nonprofit theatre company. This type of company is dedicated to creating professional theatre but operates on smaller budgets than large commercial theatres. A nonprofit theatre produces a variety of different types of performances and plays, and may have one or two musicals included in its season. Traditionally, nonprofit theatres are more affordable for their audiences and tend to do more unusual/artistic/avant-garde performances.

Decide the following:

1.) <u>DECIDE THIS FIRST.</u> It is important that you complete Step 1 before moving on because all other decisions are based on it.

What is your mission or vision for your theatre?

See these online examples: http://www.goodmantheatre.org/About/Mission.aspx, http://www.walnutstreettheatre.org/theatre/mission.php, or http://americanplayers.org/about/.

(Your mission should include the style of theatre you want to produce, who your target audience is, and what your goals are [e.g., education, community based, entertainment, political, musical].)

2.) **Where will you locate your theatre? Why?**

Location is key. If your theatre is geared toward a young 20-year-old audience, you might have better luck in a city center than in an outlying area. A theatre geared toward senior citizens might find a good home in a Florida retirement community.

3.) **What will your season of plays be?**

Your "season" refers to a couple of different issues.

a.) First, decide what months your theatre will run (August–May is a typical theatre "season" for regional theatres, but a children's theatre might be better if running in the summer when kids are out of school).

b.) Second, decide on a "season" of at least four plays that will be produced during that period. Look for plays whose genre, subject, or style fits your theatre's mission. Visit the following websites that represent the work of hundreds of different playwrights: http://www.samuelfrench.com/store/index.php, http://www.tams-witmark.com/, http://www.dramatists.com/, http://www.pioneerdrama.com/, http://www.broadwayplaypubl.com/; and http://www.mtishows.com/. (Note: Remember, musicals are very expensive, so, although they are not off limits, you probably shouldn't choose a fully musical season either.)

(List author AND title)

1.

2.

3.

4.

THE REHEARSAL PROCESS

Rebecca Morrice, Colleen Reilly, David Skeele, and Laura Smiley

CHAPTER OBJECTIVES

- Recognize that theatre is a collaborative process.
- Identify the steps in the rehearsal process.
- Understand the role of the stage manager in coordinating the rehearsal process.
- Understand the importance of communication in the rehearsal process.
- Recognize the rehearsal process as a culmination of theatre craft.

The Director/Designer Relationship

Of the many tasks the modern director performs, the trickiest is perhaps the task of coordinating and helping synthesize the work of other theatre artists. On one hand, the director is responsible for making sure the various artistic elements mesh together and serve some kind of overall vision of the play. On the other, the director is collaborating with a host of individual artists who must be allowed the freedom to work their own magic on their specific areas of production.

Imagine you are a scene designer and a director approaches you with this vision for the play: "It's a play, I think, about...love. Not romantic love, exactly, although some of it is romantic. The set should be kind of modern, and it should be lyrical, but not too lyrical (except in places). We should see some of the cynicism of the world of the play. Oh yeah, and there should be some columns somewhere." What exactly could you do with this inarticulate nonsense? You would have to do a lot of guessing about what this director meant, and there would be good chance that your fellow designers would each have a different (possibly radically different) interpretation of what the words meant.

Now imagine the director says this: "I want two octagonal columns upstage, with a round revolving platform center. Surround the platform with scaffolding that has been spray-painted hot pink, and hang a giant, fringed yellow curtain behind the columns." Nothing vague here—this is much better, right? Of course not. Actually, it's much worse. What this director has done is essentially walked up to you and said: "Here's my set. Build it for me." Not only has this director completely stifled you creatively, he has taken over an area in which he is presumably far less skilled than you, and so assured himself an inferior set.

We've now seen examples of how not to communicate with designers, but we still haven't answered the question of how a good director/designer relationship functions.

Typically, a director meets with set, lighting, costume, properties, and sound designers long before the first rehearsal (hair and make-up designers, too, sometimes). The director has prepared for the meeting by doing exhaustive readings of the script and research on the time period, place, culture, and situations contained

KEY TERMS

Cue to cue
Dress rehearsal
Stage manager
Strike
Technical rehearsal

in the play, and at these early meetings, the designers are generally content to let the director do most of the talking. There are many avenues a director might wish to explore with the designers: the particular elements of the play he or she finds exciting and thus wishes to stress, what he or she feels the play is about, the images or feelings or moods the play seems to evoke. In conducting this discussion, the director generally tries to find a middle path between the two extremes described earlier. He or she wants to convey his or her interpretation as vividly and concretely as possible, but leave up to the designers most (if not all) decisions about how to translate these ideas into actual costumes and sets and soundscapes.

Sometimes, of course, a director's interpretation often already includes some sense of how the production might look or sound, but suggestions in this regard need not be overbearing or stifling to the designers. In fact, designers often appreciate "jumping-off points" for their own ideas, and they are almost always able to transform the director's suggestions so completely that there is no question of whose artistry is being featured. As a director, I like to think of it this way: I hand the designers some ideas, they wrestle with them for a while and then hand them back to me at least five times better than they were!

As an example, a few years ago I directed Slippery Rock University's production of *Oedipus Rex*. In my initial discussions with designers, I expressed to them my desire to go far away from the usual methods of producing collegiate Greek tragedy. No rows of robed people moaning and declaiming in unison for me, thanks. I felt that the most satisfying Greek tragedy I had ever seen had been done with puppets, so I suggested an approach in which each character would be a kind of life-sized puppet, voiced by a different actor who sat at a table upstage and spoke the lines into a microphone. I also wanted a setting for the play that effectively communicated the sense of the characters being larger than life. In this post-Watergate, post-Monica Lewinsky world, we no longer view political figures as being more than human. But if our leaders are no longer the god-like beings they were in ancient Greece, what kind of people do seem larger than life to us? Athletes, perhaps, and rock stars. My choice, though, was comic superheroes. I didn't want to be too obvious, with Oedipus in tights and a cape with a huge "O" emblazoned on his chest, but I did want to strongly suggest that mythical superhero world we all believed in so desperately as children. I suggested to the designers a world fashioned after D.C. Comics of the 1940s and '50s, and then stepped back and let them work their magic.

Set and lighting designer Gordon Phetteplace came up with a menacing urban skyscape, where cut-out buildings flared at the top in cartoonish forced perspective, and bathed it in the mysterious nighttime blues and greens that once covered the pages of Batman. Costume designer Jenny Bernson fashioned (as one example) a suit for the title character with wide lapels, impossibly broad and square shoulders and a sharply tapered waist, while his full-face mask featured a jutting, square jaw and Superman's trademark forehead curl. These designs originated in some way with my interpretive ideas, but I would have been almost completely incapable of turning those ideas into a living reality, and anything I might have managed would have paled before the exquisite craftsmanship and visual imagination of these skilled artists.

It is worth noting that the working methods I describe here are typical, but there are other models for director/designer collaboration. Sometimes, it is a particular designer who conceives of an initial production element, and then the director bases his or her work on that element. For instance, a costume designer may have an interest in working with a particular kind of fabric, or in designing in a particular period, and the director allows this fabric or this period to serve as his or her own jumping-off point. In educational theatre, it is sometimes desired by scene designers and technical directors that students have experience in building different kinds of sets. So a need for an arena staging might be accepted by the director as a given, and allowed to influence the overall interpretation of the play.

The exact collaborative model is not that important. What is important is that the process is collaborative. If there is open, clear, and honest communication, and if each artist respects the parts contributed by the others, the production stands a much greater chance of forming a coherent and powerful whole.

The Stage Manager

You are probably wondering how all of this process can come together with so many different practitioners and perspectives working toward the same goal. Have you ever heard the expression "there are too many cooks in the kitchen"? While the director is the final authority on the production, the expertise of each of the practitioners is mutually respected. In order to be sure that there is clear communication and organization of ideas it is absolutely necessary that a **stage manager** be in place throughout the rehearsal process.

The stage manager has the full responsibility for the execution of the production from its conception to its life on stage. They are present in preliminary meetings, at auditions, throughout the rehearsal process, and for every performance during a production run. This is because they must ensure that the vision of the director and designers is faithfully performed every time. The stage manager undertakes a variety of activities to successfully run smooth production meetings, rehearsals, and production meetings.

In my experience as a stage manager it is very important to be conscientious, organized, and good natured. You have to listen very closely to the concerns of the director, designers, and actors and work proactively towards a solution. This occurs in very small production scenarios such as when a prop is misplaced onstage, to serious personal issues like the replacement of an injured actor.

The stage manager takes detailed production notes during rehearsal and distributes them to everyone involved in the production staff. They collect cue sheets from each of the designers and assemble them into a master prompt book which also contains the production script. The promptbook is comprised of the cues, blocking, rehearsal schedules, contact information, ground plans, and numerous other essential documents for the production. It is often referred to as the production "bible."

A good stage manager is part referee, part nanny, and part prison warden. She must be able to keep lines of communication clear, nurture the artists involved in the process, and be very firm about deadlines, schedules, and expectations. With a stage manager in place the production staff can trust that they are working in a safe and controlled environment. The director and designers can be confident that their choices will be respected. And the actors are reassured that the things needed for their performance will be in place. The continuity that a stage manager brings to the rehearsal process allows everyone to be creative!

The Rehearsal Process

Rehearsal is a time of discovery! An intricate dance of give and take among the actor, the director, and the ensemble. Frequently the first rehearsal is the first time the director and the cast have been together. Introductions all around, business from the stage manager, words from the director and then...the first read-through. This is the first time that this play has been read with this particular group of actors for this particular production of the play. The first read-through is not about the acting, it is about listening—to the words, their rhythm and cadences, the voices of the ensemble, the story. After the read-through, there is table work: discussion and questioning about the text, the characters, the concept. This is where the foundation is laid.

I find table work especially crucial in doing Shakespeare. We look up words when we are not sure of their meaning, and literary, mythological, and geographical references. At this point the designers often join the table. The scene designer may bring a model, the costume designer renderings. This helps the actors visualize and actively imagine the world of the play, which helps them interpret and construct their characters. On a more practical level, it gives them an idea of how many steps it might take to cross the stage or climb the steps or what freedom or constraint their costumes allow. From here on, the process differs from director to director.

While the director and the actors are working on blocking and characterization in rehearsals, the designers and their teams are involved in the process of bringing their ideas to life as well. The designers continue to meet with the director, the stage manager keeps the designers and technicians informed of changes made during rehearsals, the designers collaborate with one another to make sure their work will mesh together, and the technicians are building in their respective shops.

During the production process, the costume designer will be making and finding costumes and scheduling fittings with the actors. The prop master will be providing rehearsal props for the actors to work with, while also making and finding the props that will be used in the actual performance. The technical director will be building the sets. While all of these activities may be happening in the same building or in separate locations across town, eventually everyone will come back together for *first tech* which is the *first technical rehearsal* when the set, lights, props, and sound are all integrated into the actors' and director's process.

Some theatre companies choose to introduce costumes at this time too; others will wait a few more days before actors "dress" for the first time. If they choose to wait to introduce the costumes, *first dress* will usually happen within a few days of first tech once the technical elements have been adjusted and set. For everyone, first dress is when finally begin to see and understand what the finished production will be like. It is a very exciting and exhausting process!

What is true to all rehearsal processes, is that it is a vital time of exploration and discovery necessary to bring the page to the stage in a creative fashion. As opening night approaches new elements are added during tech week. In these **technical rehearsals**, the lights, scenery, and sound cues become integrated.

Before an actual technical run, there is usually something called a **cue to cue**. This is the rehearsal when all the technical elements come together for the first time. The actors are asked to be patient as the designers and technical staff run the production literally from cue to cue: from one lighting cue to a sound cue to a scene change. It is during this time that sound and light levels are set and scene changes are choreographed. Once these aspects are in place, there will be several runs of the play with these components added to rehearse the calling of technical cues and for the actors to acclimate to these new elements. And then there are the **dress rehearsals**: this is when the actors wear their costumes for the first time. This completes the technical cycle of the rehearsal process. This is an exciting time for the actors—the costumes are the finishing touches of character development. It should be noted here that often during the rehearsal process, actors will be given rehearsal costumes to work with, especially if the play is a period piece. I frequently ask the costume designer for shoes for my actors—I find that shoes help with creating the physicality of the character. Think about it: you move quite differently depending on whether you are wearing sneakers or high heels or dress oxfords!

Depending on the production schedule, preview performances follow. This completes the circle, the final piece of the puzzle without which there would be no theatre: the audience! At this time, the audience is invited to experience the production before its scheduled opening. During these performances, adjustments are made to make the play more effective. It can be technical, for example raising or lowering the sound levels; or it can be about pacing and rhythm of the scenes. Very often, there are post-show discussions to elicit responses from the audience about what was effective and perhaps what was not. In any case it is a period during which adjustments can be made before the opening night when the critics arrive!

And finally it is here! This moment is the purpose of all the actor's training and the foundation built during the exhilarating and challenging rehearsal process. A well-rehearsed play provides the actor with the control and confidence to give a fully realized, totally energized performance. It provides the actor with the skills to be open to audience response as well as being able and prepared to adjust to any unexpected surprises that invariably happen in live performances. The final challenge once the play opens is for the actor to find ways to continually be true to the character and the world of the play, and to be fresh and in the moment whether the play runs for three days, three weeks, three months or three years!

The production **strike** is the final step in the rehearsal and production process. The set is disassembled and either destroyed or stored. Costumes are returned to stock or recycled. Props are stored, sound and lighting equipment disassembled, and scripts are returned to the publisher.

Conclusion

The rehearsal process is a dynamic time when all theatre practitioners engage in the process of making meaning in the theatre. This collaborative, deadline oriented, and creative process is one of the most unique features of theatrical art. As the process moves from auditions towards performance each participant is in constant communication about the work of bringing a unique performance to the stage through the dedicated efforts of everyone involved.

Suggested Exercises

Select a play mentioned in the course textbook and read it carefully.

Imagine that you are preparing a proposal for the production of this play. Your objective is to convince the reader to stage your production. Use citations from the text as needed to support your argument.

Prepare a one- to two-page analysis that must contain the following:

- Paragraph 1: A thesis statement that introduces your reasons for proposing the production.
- Paragraph 2: Describe the playwright's use of plot, character, and language.
- Paragraph 3: Identify the major character(s) and their objective(s).
- Paragraph 4: Create a concept for the production of the play from the viewpoint of a director.
- Paragraph 5: Provide a compelling and convincing conclusion to persuade the reader to stage your proposed production.

EVALUATING THEATRE

Theatrical practice can be found in every record of human civilization. Early documentation of theatrical activity shows a connection to community rituals and sacred rites. For centuries, scholars have traced the origins of modern theatre to religious festivals in Greece, but other evidence suggests that Egyptian ceremonies predate these Greek dramatic competitions. Part of the problem in defining the origins of theatre is that we have new ways of thinking about history itself.

For theatre historians and practitioners, this means that we must examine all manifestations of theatre, not just those represented in traditional history texts. We cannot rely on an easy chronology of European theatre, because we now understand that contemporary to someone like William Shakespeare were playwrights and practitioners in Africa, Asia, and South America who were equally sophisticated. It is a thrilling moment in theatrical history because now, unlike in previous eras, we can be fully aware of the theatrical practice in other cultures. We can study it, experience it, and even incorporate it into our production choices!

This unit has four chapters: Theatre Criticism, Elements of the Drama, Theatrical Forms, and Global Theatrical Forms. Each chapter will engage and discuss how historical thinking about theatre shapes contemporary theatre-making for practitioners.

THEATRE CRITICISM

Colleen Reilly

CHAPTER OBJECTIVES

- To understand the difference between evaluating a play and evaluating a production.
- To complete a process of theatrical analysis.
- To identify production choices.
- To feel confident evaluating a performance.
- To complete a written review of a production.

Play Versus Production

As discussed in Chapter 1, the Audience is one of the four fundamental elements of theatre. Chapter 1 defined theatre as a social transaction and discussed the tension between an active and passive audience. This chapter explores further your role in making meaning in the theatre. You may have heard the expression "everyone's a critic," but what does that mean for theatrical criticism? What are the steps in evaluating a production? This chapter discusses the process of theatrical analysis.

Before we begin to evaluate the art of theatrical criticism, it is crucial that we distinguish between dramatic analysis and production analysis. Theatrical productions are often (but not always) based on an interpretation of a play. It is important in theatrical criticism to separate your analysis of that text from its realization on the stage. You might like the play, but dislike the staging, or vice versa. Although it is perfectly acceptable to have preconceived notions about the meaning of a particular play or text, it is CRITICAL that you treat your analysis of a production on its own terms.

For example, Norwegian playwright Henrik Ibsen wrote *A Doll's House* in 1879. Nineteenth-century audiences were scandalized when the play's central character, Nora, stormed out of her house at the end of the play, abandoning her husband and family for her own sense of self-realization. This theatrical moment was called "The Door Slam Heard 'Round the World," and many theatres protested this radical action and demanded a revision to the play that kept this character safe within the confines of her role as wife and mother. This reaction was due entirely to the play itself, and the criticism was pointed at the playwright for creating this dangerous scenario.

Flash forward over a century and *A Doll's House* has become one of the most celebrated plays of all time. It is required reading for many secondary and post-secondary schools, and is generally considered an example of superior playwriting. In 2003, avant-garde director Lee Breuer adapted the play for the stage and cast average-sized actors in female roles and diminutive actors in male roles. Audiences were scandalized, this time because of the production choice.

KEY TERMS

Eclecticism
Ephemeral
Motif
Representative quote
Suspension of disbelief
Theatrical event

Theatrical Analysis

When scholars look at theatre from an academic perspective, we like to organize theatrical styles and forms into neat historical periods. This helps us define how theatre was made in different cultures at different times, what purposes it may have served, and to what extent it was valued by the cultures that produced it. We imagine, for example, that the classical Greek society valued theatre given the amount of effort it would have taken to carve theatrical spaces out of hillsides. However, this kind of periodization is completely frustrated by current theatrical practice. Contemporary theatre is marked most by **eclecticism**, or the combination of numerous styles.

How then do you, the contemporary audience member, go about evaluating a theatrical production? The strategy that I suggest and most often use as a starting place involves posing a series of three questions borrowed from the 18th-century German playwright Johann Wolfgang von Goethe:

1. What is the artist trying to do?
2. How well is the artist doing it?
3. Is it worth doing?

Let's begin with the first question, "What is the artist trying to do?" The first thing we must do is ask ourselves, "Who is the artist in question?" A theatrical production involves the craft of numerous artists: the director, the designers, and the actors. That artistry deserves to be considered on its own terms, but to take each practitioner individually could prove to be a lengthy and difficult process.

Instead, we tend to consider the organizing principle of the production to respond to the first question, and usually this comes from the directorial concept. Thus, one way to discuss the production as a whole may be to ask, "What is the director trying to do?" This allows you to focus on the total performance while providing some room to work through an analysis of the other practitioners, because we can assume that they are working under the guidance of the director.

Please note, however, that some productions are more collaborative or ensemble based. In these cases, it might be useful to ask, "What is the production trying to do?" Framing the question in this way recognizes that everyone involved is working toward a common goal. There is no hard-and-fast rule about which type of production lends itself to which question, but if you have trouble answering one, you might consider posing the other.

In either case, it might feel strange to think about theatre "doing" something. Theatre attempts to do many things. It strives to teach, to entertain, to inspire, to provoke, to investigate, to comfort, and to remember—the list is as infinite as human experience. But thinking about the cause and effect of theatre is incredibly important to this process of interpretation. In theatre, the answer to "What is the artist trying to do?" is really "What has the artist done to me?" Because we can never really know what someone else's intentions might have been, we can only measure the evidence of theatre "doing" something through our own experience.

You might find yourself sitting through a performance and thinking, "The artist must be trying to bore me," but I would invite you to dig a little deeper.

Is the action slow-paced, is the design monochromatic, and the acting subdued? Are any of these the evidence of a directorial concept or a production choice? Or perhaps you find yourself in a performance with confrontational acting, in an intimate audience configuration, with provocative costumes. You might conclude that the artist is trying to make you feel something. The answer to the question, "What is the artist trying to do?" lies in the observations you make about the way that your experience is being framed. When you base your response in the relationship between what is happening onstage and what is happening to you, you are ready for the next question: "How well is the artist doing it?"

In previous chapters, we have discussed the craft of the major collaborators of the theatre. This should provide some insight into how an artist achieves his or her artistic (and professional) goals. When you engage the events onstage with an inquisitive attitude, you are truly participating in the social transaction of theatre. Artists in the theatre want the audience to think, to feel, and to experience. Notice that there are two facets of the second question in theatrical criticism. You need not only to identify the "how" of the artists' work by locating artist choices, but also to evaluate "how well." You might be a little hesitant to judge an artist's performance, but let's walk through these steps together.

Production Choices

Let's look first at the choices that the artists are making in theatrical production. One way I like to approach this is by asking, "What choices have been made here?" Make a mental note of what you see and feel that resonates with you. You may later discover that other people in the audience share your observation, and it can be important to contextualize your experience in terms of what you observe in other audience reactions. The choices that you identify in the production elements will shape your evaluation of the performance. Here are some questions to get you started:

Director	Is there a directorial concept? How has the director organized the production elements?
Actor	What are the actors doing? Does it appear natural or stylized?
Playwright	What kind of story is the playwright showing? Is the conflict real or is it imagined?
Scenic Design	What is the world of the play? How would you describe the aesthetic?
Costume Design	What are the actors wearing? How do the costumes enhance your understanding of the character?
Lighting Design	What kind of atmosphere is being created by the lighting? Are there particular cues that get your attention?
Sound Design	Is the sound ambient? What tone is set by the use of sound cues?

Another strategy to identify choices in production is to look for *theatrical effects*. A theatrical effect can be anything you see, feel, or hear in a production that conveys a meaning to the audience. As you might suspect, the recognition of theatrical effects can be a very subjective process. This is why it can be helpful to discuss the performance with other audience members during intermission or after the show. If a talkback with the actors, directors, or technicians is scheduled, you might consider sharing your observations and posing questions directly to the artists. Contemporary theatres are constantly striving to create more opportunities for dialogue with their audiences.

Once you have made a mental note of the choices, ask yourself, "Why these choices, and not others?" Is an actor moving in a particular way, is there a light cue that is being repeated, are you noticing a specific color being used over and over? Any recurrent theme or design element in a production can be referred to as a **motif**. The use of motifs is one way that a director can organize production elements or highlight a particular image, metaphor, or symbol. Motifs can help you map out a particular interpretation. They can also help you construct a theory or thesis about "why" some choices are made and not others.

This leads to the final question in Goethe's process of analysis: "Is it worth doing?" This too can be a very complicated and subjective question. Clearly, the artists committed to the performance have invested time, energy, and creativity in the process. This would suggest that they feel it is worth doing. It is likely that you are not sitting alone in the audience, so other people have elected to spend time engaging the performance; therefore, they must think it is worth doing. Ultimately, you must take your own position in response to this question. You should approach your response thoughtfully and be prepared to support your ideas with evidence from the production itself.

Theatrical Reviews

Theatrical art is **ephemeral**. Performances are impermanent, and no two performances are identical. This is one of the reasons that theatrical reviews are so important: They serve as a record of what transpired in the theatre in a particular time and place. It is important to take your responsibility as a documentarian seriously; you must try to be objective, descriptive, and demonstrate some insight into theatrical craft all in one go.

When you attend a theatrical performance, it is important to engage in what poet Samuel Coleridge described as "the **suspension of disbelief**." This state of mind refers to your willingness to overlook reality in favor of an illusion. It also refers to your ability to allow the stagecraft of a play to disappear into theatricality. For example, you look past the proscenium stage once the play begins and accept that the action is happening in the world of the play. If a character is meant "to fly," you accept that he is "flying" once his feet leave the ground, even though you know it is the stage machinery and not a magical apparatus that is making this happen. The suspension of disbelief is a key element not only to your enjoyment of a performance, but also to your ability to be objective.

This may seem like a contradiction; however, the suspension of disbelief allows you to move past the obvious questions and work from inside the production. It helps you to be sensitive to a play's possibilities and critical of a production's shortcomings. As much fun as it can be to write a love letter or a rant about a particular production, a good review is balanced and descriptive.

It is also very much based on what you observed onstage rather than your expectations, memories, or personal biases. Following is the structure of a review that I recommend:

Heading: Your name, date, and time of performance attended

Paragraph 1: State your thesis about the production, based on your conclusions to Goethe's questions. I recommend also using a **representative quote** from the play. A representative quote is a line, speech, or production image that summarizes what you see as the meaning of the production. This will help orient your reader to your point of view and establish your response on the play's terms. It will also shape your thesis, because this representative quote will provide a way into what you have noticed about the play. Your introduction should identify the name of the production, playwright, and production company, along with the date and location.

Paragraph 2: Describe the observations that led to your thesis on the production in terms of the artist's production choices. Start by naming the Director and addressing the directorial concept. Evaluate whether any differences exist between the play and the production. Discuss the other practitioner choices and name key actors and designers.

Paragraph 3: Describe the production's conventions, motifs, and theatrical effects. Identify how these production elements support your thesis. Be as graphic and expressive as possible.

Paragraph 4: Report the audience's overall response to the production. Make any final comments about the stagecraft. Revisit your representative quote and conclude the review.

Conclusion

This chapter provides a process of theatrical analysis and a template for a production review to prepare you for your role as critic. But there are many more considerations to make when approaching the eclecticism of contemporary theatres. The next chapters will discuss the dramatic forms and theatrical styles you might experience in current theatrical practice. The most important element of theatrical analysis is that you feel informed about the process and the possibilities of theatrical art.

Suggested Exercise: Representative Quotes

Your course instructor will provide excerpts from a play and describe elements of its staged production. Choose a representative quote from the text provided and create a 1-minute essay that uses that quote to comment on the production. This is an imaginary review for an imaginary production: Be creative!

ELEMENTS OF THE DRAMA
Colleen Reilly

CHAPTER OBJECTIVES

- By the end of this chapter, students will be able to describe Aristotle's dramatic elements.
- By the end of this chapter, students will be able to identify common features of dramatic plots.

Aristotle defined six elements of the drama: plot, character, thought, language, music, and spectacle. We still tend to organize our thinking about the theatre using these tools. Although Aristotle was writing specifically about *tragedy*, which he defined as the *imitation of an action*, we use his elements of the drama to describe many different genres of theatrical creations.

Aristotle outlines his dramatic theory in the *Poetics*, and he not only defines the six elements but also describes how they work together to create a theatrical moment. Let's start by discussing the six dramatic elements.

Plot	Thought
Character	Language
Spectacle	Music

Plot

The plot is the organization of the action of the play, or the sequence of events that tells the story. Often, we confuse the terms *plot* and *story*. In casual conversations, we tend to use these terms interchangeably. We use expressions like "that's my story and I'm sticking to it" and "the plot thickens." In both of these examples, we are talking about basically the same thing; that is, the narrative that we are constructing about a specific event.

When we discuss "plot" as it relates to theatre and drama, we refer to the organization of the narrative. Every story has a beginning, a middle, and an end; however, we can "plot" the story by starting in different places. For example, *Betrayal* by Harold Pinter tells the story of an adulterous affair. The opening scene is set in 1977 at the end of the relationship. The final scene is set in 1968 when the lovers first meet. This way of organizing or plotting the events of the narrative is referred to as **reverse chronology**.

In David Henry Hwang's *M. Butterfly*, the opening stage directions note, "The action of the play takes place in a Paris prison in the present, and in recall during the decade 1960–1970 in Beijing, and from 1966 to the present in Paris." This is what we refer to as a **nonlinear plot**. The events of the play shift between the past and the present, and the manipulation of time becomes part of the playwright's strategy of creating the sequence of the plot.

Some common features of plots contribute to a dramatic text: point of attack, exposition, and climax. **Point of attack** refers to the place where the playwright begins the action of the play. In the previous examples, the point of attack disrupted chronological time. **Exposition** provides anything the audience needs to know to understand the play. It often describes the past with details about events leading up to the point of attack. The **climax** of the play is the emotional high point of the plot. It contains the moment of reversal or change in the action. The tension in the plot is usually heightened to a breaking point, and the scenes that follow show the resolution of the plot.

Conflict is also a common feature of dramatic plots. The conflict of the play occurs when two or more forces are working against each other. The conflict creates obstacles that characters must overcome to move the action along and achieve a goal.

There are many ways to describe conflict, but perhaps the most useful way to think about it for theatrical practice is in terms of internal conflict and external conflict. Internal conflict refers to a contradiction arising from within a main character, usually the protagonist. Hamlet's famous soliloquy from Act 3, Scene I illuminates internal conflict. Hamlet's indecision prevents him from taking action to avenge his father's death.

> To be, or not to be: that is the question:
> Whether 'tis nobler in the mind to suffer
> The slings and arrows of outrageous fortune,
> Or to take arms against a sea of troubles,
> And by opposing end them? (*Hamlet*, 3.1)

The external conflict in drama comes from whatever it is that forces the protagonist or main character to overcome an obstacle. The antagonist or opposition to the main character is usually the source of the external conflict. In Hamlet's case, the antagonist is his uncle, Claudius. Claudius forces Hamlet into an endgame scenario by the end of the play. Some of the most powerful conflicts in dramatic texts occur between two opposing characters.

Character

Very simply put, a character is a representation of a human being. In theatre, a character can be realized through many different means including actors, puppets, and virtual environments. Characters can be portrayed as deeply complex individuals or "**stock characters**."

Stock characters are stereotypical or overly generalized character types. They evolve from commedia dell'arte, an improvisatory form of theatre from the Italian Renaissance that was based around a hierarchy of characters including wily servants, overbearing masters, and star-crossed lovers.

In dramatic texts, characters are referred to as dramatis personae, or persons in the play. Aristotle's *Poetics* tells us that "Character is that which reveals moral purpose, showing what kind of things a man chooses or avoids."[1] If we take both of these ways of thinking about character together, we can establish that as a dramatic element, characters become the vehicles for the dramatic action.

Because dramatic action often revolves around conflicts, we usually think about character in terms of the protagonist and antagonist. The *protagonist* is the main character of the play, and the plot often revolves around his or her interests. An *antagonist* is a secondary character who creates obstacles that the protagonist must overcome. Similar to plots, the conflict between the antagonist and protagonist can be internal or external. Conflict is a key element in both plot and character.

Many modern and contemporary plays feature ensemble casts rather than individual protagonists. Ensemble casts feature characters with relatively equal stage time and importance to the plot. Ensembles generally appear in comedies and musicals; however, contemporary theatre business models encourage ensemble casting, and this has led to the development of more serious dramatic use of ensembles. *Clybourne Park* is one contemporary example of a serious play with an ensemble cast. Written in 2010 by Bruce Norris, *Clybourne Park* revisits the world of Lorraine Hansberry's *A Raisin in the Sun* to explore contemporary racial issues. Ensemble casts in serious plays often shift the focus from personal or individual issues to more political or social ideas.

Thought

All plays contain a purpose, argument, or organizing idea. Aristotle described this feature as the "thought" of the play. It can be very easy to confuse the "plot" of the play and the "thought" of the play. For example, Arthur Miller's play *The Crucible* is set in New England during the Salem witch trials. It might be easy to assume that this play is "about" witches. However, if we look more closely at the context of the play, we might arrive at a different conclusion as to what the play is about. Miller wrote this play in 1952 during the McCarthy era when many artists were subjected to interrogation and persecution under suspicion of communist activities. Miller uses the 1692 witch trials as an allegory for the "witch hunt" of the Red Scare. These historical events inform the plot of *The Crucible*, but we can say that the "thought" of the play points to broader questions of the danger conspiracy and social anxieties.

Language

Theatrical language always straddles between prose and poetry. When we look at texts from different historical periods, we can examine their use of poetic devices such as meter, rhythm, and rhyme. In Aristotle's classical theatre, the lines of text would have been sung, and are therefore naturally poetic. Shakespeare wrote in the poetic form of **iambic pentameter** as one of the conventions of Elizabethan drama. It was not until late in the 19th century that plays began featuring vernacular, or everyday, speech as part of the impact of realism in theatrical practice.

---

[1]Aristotle. *Poetics*. New York: Cosimo, 2008: 13.

Iambic pentameter is a structure of verse containing a line with five beats. In each beat there is a stressed accent and an unstressed accent, which creates a rhythm that resembles the human heartbeat. It was commonly used in Shakespeare's time. Try reading this line from Shakespeare's *Richard III* with your heartbeat in mind ("lub dub, lub dub, lub dub, lub dub, lub dub"): "Now is / the win / ter of/ our dis/ con tent."

Three of the major forms of language used in theatre are prose, verse, and blank verse. Prose refers to everyday speech and is the predominant form of contemporary dramatic language. Modern audiences tend to enjoy the expectation that characters onstage will sound like they do, using familiar words, phrases, and expressions. However, this has not always been the case.

Historically, audiences have shared an expectation that a playwright was composing dramatic texts within a specific poetic form. Classical theatre was written in verse, as were most plays through the nineteenth century. Playwrights conformed to the poetic conventions of the time and used rhyming lines or blank verse, that is, nonrhyming lines that maintain a particular meter.

Classical tragedies are often translated into blank verse. Classical comedies are usually translated into rhyming verse. This can make it extremely difficult and unpleasant to read these plays, but it is an attempt to capture the musicality of the original Greek and Roman texts.

Recently, contemporary plays have shown an interest in reincorporating poetic and musical forms into dramatic texts. Many playwrights draw on jazz, hip-hop, and spoken word to form the lines of their plays. These playwrights are often as interested in the sound of the words that they use as much as their meaning. Sam Shepard and Suzan Lori Parks are two playwrights who deliberately "play" with these forms.

Music

Of Aristotle's dramatic elements, music is perhaps the most difficult for a contemporary audience to grasp. We have a long history of musical theatre and might easily assume that Aristotle's "music" refers the same kind of musical experience. However, Aristotle's musical dramatic element more closely describes the mood or atmosphere of the play.

In classical theatre, most of the text was sung; therefore, Aristotle's consideration of music would have included thinking about the characteristics of harmony, rhythm, and melody. These features would have impacted the audience's mood and emotional response to the play. Over time and as the language of theatre became more prose based, we can trace the transition of these "musical" features into a more general "feeling" of the play. The level of conflict relates to the classical notion of harmony. The pace of a scene speaks to the rhythm. Aristotle's melody can be traced in the tone of the scene.

Spectacle

The final dramatic element in our discussion is spectacle. Spectacle refers to all of the visual elements of the production. For Aristotle, spectacle was the least important dramatic element. New we tend to see it from a more balanced perspective and recognize the artistry of scenic, light, and costume design. We also recognize that spectacle can be central to the experience of the "seeing place" of the theatre. Contemporary playwrights are sometimes very deliberate about the realization of the visual elements of their plays. For example, in the stage directions of *Angels in America* playwright Tony Kushner states:

> The play benefits from a pared-down style of presentation, with minimal scenery and scene shifts done rapidly (no blackouts!) employing the cast as well as stagehands–which makes for an actor-driven event, as this must be. The moments of magic–the appearance and disappearance of Mr. Lies and the ghosts, the book hallucination, and the ending–are to be fully realised, as bits of wonderful Theatrical illusion–which means it's OK if the wires show, and maybe it's good that they do, but the magic should at the same time be thoroughly amazing.[2]

For Kushner, theatrical spectacle is minimal, but magical. The poetry of the spectacle occurs in its execution.

Conclusion

Aristotle's dramatic elements give us a consistent way to address the dramatic and theatrical content of the text of any given performance. In 5th century Greece those texts existed in two forms: tragedy and comedy. In 2012 "performance" has expanded to mean just about anything that contains the fundamental units of theatre. It is thrilling that we can reach back millennia to Aristotle's dramatic theory to organize our thinking about theatrical craft. In the next chapters we will begin to discuss many of the dramatic and theatrical forms that have evolved over that time.

Works Cited

Hwang, David Henry. *M. Butterfly*. New York, Plume, 1989.

---

[2]Kushner, Tony. *Angels in America*. New York: TCG, 1993.

THEATRICAL FORMS

Colleen Reilly and Deb Cohen

CHAPTER OBJECTIVES

- To recognize the characteristics of different genres used in the contemporary theatre.
- To identify the characteristics of different theatrical styles.
- To perceive theatrical productions as the result of stylistic choices.

All art has developed over time into various recognizable forms and styles. Theatre is no different from other visual, literary, or performing arts in this respect. In fact, the discipline of theatre freely borrows from other artistic disciplines and incorporates elements of historical, modern, and contemporary styles from all forms of human expression, often in a single production. How then is a contemporary audience meant to prepare to "get" what theatre artists are trying to accomplish with these stylistic choices? This chapter provides some basic information about theatrical genre and styles that you are likely to see incorporated into today's theatre practice.

Theatrical Genre

Contemporary theatre practice is not overly concerned with strict definitions of **genre**, but historically, very strict rules were in place that defined the two major forms of dramatic art. For centuries, theatrical entertainments were assigned as either belonging to the category of tragedy or comedy. These forms may have originated from very specific rites that celebrated the Greek god Dionysus. Scholars believe that these ancient songs and dances evolved into the playwriting competitions that defined the classical era of theatre.

During the Renaissance there was renewed interest in the classical forms of art, which may have reintroduced rigid structures and expectations of these two genres. However, the Renaissance worldview was very different from that of the classical Greek and Roman societies and some alterations were made. Throughout recorded history there have been attempts to define, regulate, and evaluate artistic practice. Aristotle, Horace, Cicero, Dante, Cervantes, Shakespeare, Goethe, Voltaire, Freud, Ibsen, Nietzsche, Brecht, and numerous others have contributed to a vast pool of theatrical criticism. Contemporary theatre takes a very eclectic view of these classifications, but you are likely to see productions that broadly fall into three genres: Tragedy, Comedy, or Musical Theatre.

> *Genre:* A category of art that complies with particular rules of form.

KEY TERMS

Agitprop
Book musicals
Chitlin' circuit
Comedy
Dark comedy
Devised theatre
Domestic comedy
Epic theatre
Genre
Historical practices
Horror
Improvisation
Jukebox musicals
Lazzi
Melodrama
Metatragedy
Musical theatre
Nonrealism
Poor theatre
Realism
Theatre of cruelty
Theatre of the absurd
Theatre of the oppressed
Tragedy

Tragedy

Tragedy is perhaps one of the most overused words in the English language. It is crucial for this discussion to divorce our everyday sensibility of the word from the use of the genre of tragedy in theatrical art. Theatrical tragedy originated as the reversal of fortune because of a character's fatal flaw. This reversal of fortune might result in death, dismemberment, or banishment. It is often referred to as the fall, or the rapid descent from power or grace. The fatal flaw may be described as pride, or a willful error in judgment. Theatrical tragedy, therefore, excludes external causes of sad or disastrous events. The "tragedy" is driven by human nature.

Theatrical tragedy is meant to result in *catharsis*, or the purging of emotions through pity and fear. Catharsis is intended to affect a change on the audience. We follow the dramatic action and often anticipate the reversal of fortune before the tragic hero begins to understand his or her fate. Catharsis is achieved through the relief that we experience when the hero comes to know what we already know.

My best example of catharsis comes from Euripides' *The Bacchae*. The tragic hero is Pentheus, a prince of Thebes, who has refused to allow his people to worship the god Dionysus. (This was a pretty bold choice for Euripides to make Dionysus a character in the play that he had written for a festival celebrating Dionysus.) In the climax of the play, Pentheus's mother, Agave, has returned from celebrating the rites of Dionysus. She believes that she has bravely slain a lion with her bare hands. What the audience can see and she comes to understand is that she has actually murdered her own son and is holding his severed head. The tension builds through the dramatic monologue where she realizes her mistake.

—Colleen Reilly

Tragedy has worked best in cultural periods when society at large has shared a fairly cohesive worldview. The pressure of common beliefs in divine law heightens the stakes for tragic heroes. Classical tragedy is rampant with vindictive gods and strict social structures. These tend to limit the choices that a classical hero can make. Even if Oedipus could get over his domestic issues, he could not possibly continue to rule Thebes after the scandal of incest. Renaissance tragedy is more humanistic, but still defined by social convention and the expectations of the monarchy. Hamlet is a prince, after all, and plotting to kill a king not only violates divine right but results in the upheaval of the social order.

Modern culture participates in a more individualized view of cosmic order. We live in a society that embraces many different worldviews. We have a cultural tradition that acknowledges the possibility of a separation of church and state. Any relationship that we profess to have with divine law is likely to be private or shared among our own congregation, rather than assumed to be universal.

As a result, classical tragedy has become somewhat problematic for modern and contemporary theatrical practice. Rather than seeing our place in the world as predetermined and fixed, we tend to imagine our lives as being fluid and open to possibilities. The reversals of fortune and fatal flaws of many 20th-century plays occur without the rigid social structures and belief systems of earlier historical periods. These plays can be discussed as **metatragedy**, or tragedies about the nature of tragedy in the contemporary world.

I would like to offer two different examples of metatragedy. One, Pirandello's *Six Characters in Search of an Author*, is highly philosophical. Written in 1921, it investigates the idea of individual reality. The action takes place during a theatre rehearsal that is interrupted by six individuals who claim to be characters. There are many debates about the roles that we play in our lives, and the appearance of the "characters" calls into question the already compromised reality of the "actors." (The actors are pretending to be other people, after all.) A second example of metatragedy would be Arthur Miller's *Death of a Salesman*. Miller's 1949 play focuses on an average traveling salesman, Willy Loman. This passage from the close of Act I speaks to Miller's treatment of this everyday character as a serious theatrical subject:

> I don't say he's a great man. Willie Loman never made a lot of money. His name was never in the paper. He's not the finest character that ever lived. But he's a human being, and a terrible thing is happening to him. So attention must be paid. He's not to be allowed to fall in his grave like an old dog. Attention, attention must finally be paid to such a person (40).

—Colleen Reilly

The mid-20th century also gave rise to a kind of tragedy that can be described as **theatre of the absurd**. The phrase was coined by Martin Esslin in 1960, in response to a form of theatre emerging from playwrights like Eugene Ionesco and Samuel Beckett. Perhaps the most famous play in this form is Beckett's *Waiting for Godot* (1953). The dramatic action of this play was famously described by literary critic Vivian Mercier as a play in which "nothing happens, twice."

Waiting for Godot depicts two vagrants who meet on a country road and proceed to wait for the arrival of the mysterious figure, Godot. The action, or inaction, of the play revolves around filling up the time while the two wait. As with much of the theatre of the absurd, the play is marked by the attempt to make meaning where there appears to be an absence of it.

The theatre of the absurd, as Howard Quackenbush points out, is one genre that Latin American dramatists did not copy from Europeans. In fact, Quackenbush reminds us that "from a Latin American perspective, the absurd (the irrational, inhumane, suffering, chaotic, unintelligible) forms part of everyday social life for a multitude of people in Latin American countries.... In several parts of Latin America, the Theatre of the Absurd reflects the reality of their existence" (10, my translation).[1] On the other hand, several Argentine playwrights have rejected the term *absurd* in favor of *grotesque*, to emphasize the critical aspects of their theatre, and differentiate it and separate it from European influence.

—Deb Cohen

Not all modern plays working in the genre of tragedy deny the existence of meaning or the influence of cosmic order. **Horror** plays often rely on the real presence of the supernatural. In many horror plays, the fatal flaw is expressed in the character's denial of the existence of supernatural forces. The reversal of fortune manifests itself when those forces can no longer be denied. For example, in David Skeele's *The Barwell Prophecy*, the protagonist exhausts all rational explanations before succumbing to the reality of the supernatural. In true tragic form, this mistake costs him his life.

---

[1]Quackenbush, L. Howard. *Teatro del absurdo hispanoamericano*. Mexico City: Editorial Patria, S.A., 1987. Print.

Comedy

If tragedy is a genre that pits individuals against cosmic forces, **comedy** is a genre that pits individuals against each other. The conflict between these opposing forces is often amusing, and even more often reveals the potential ridiculousness of social institutions. The genre of comedy demands that the hero must solve a problem (often contrived), and it depicts a hero that is often ill-equipped to accomplish this goal.

Like Greek tragedy, comedy is believed to have originated in celebrations of Dionysus. However, unlike the rites that evolved into tragic drama, comedy may have evolved from satyr plays-obscene celebrations of sexuality, fertility, and appetite. As cultures changed, so did the ways that these human impulses were represented. Thus, in the Renaissance and after, most comic plays concluded their action with weddings, feasts, or other moderate and socially prescribed celebrations.

Rather than seeking catharsis, comedy maintains the goal of laughter. As a result, the comic genre is often formulaic not only in its course of action from conflict to resolution, but also in the scenarios that move this action along. We often refer to **lazzi**, "comic bits," or familiar conventions that signal an audience to laugh at a character. Watching someone fall down really shouldn't be that funny; however, add a banana peel and we all have permission to laugh.

Lazzi: stock comic bits or scenarios that are often repeated.

Comedy often pokes fun at social conventions and classes. Comedies that revolve around family matters are known as **domestic comedies** and usually probe questions of marriage or paternity. Comedies that revolve around social classes are referred to as comedy of manners; they came into vogue in the late 18th century and dominated the genre to the 20th century as the middle class rose and gained social power.

In the late 1800s, budding independent nations in Latin America explored their own national character in a style known as *costumbrismo*. This theatre was entertaining and generally made fun of rural folks. Audiences were generally city dwellers with a high level of education. Even after independence from Spain, theatre companies in Latin America continued to imitate Spanish theatre to the extent that they adopted Castilian accents when they spoke onstage! (This would be the equivalent of our tendency to use English accents when acting Shakespeare.) These companies were generally run by the star actor or actress and were cast into types: the leading man, the leading lady, an older male authority figure (called *barba* after the beard he generally wore), supporting actors who played servants or family members, among others. Actors rehearsed for only a few weeks before staging new shows, and they relied heavily on prompters. Prompters were positioned under the stage at the front, with their heads inside a little shell so that the audience couldn't see them. They had the complete script and fed actors their lines when they forgot them.

Historically, comedy has consistently provided the opportunity to critique social or political positions. For modern and contemporary theatre, this has led to **dark comedy**, or gallows humor. Dark comedy uses comic scenarios to confront serious social and personal issues. Like the theatre of the absurd, dark comedy considers questions of the possibility of finding the meaning of life in the modern world.

Currently, contemporary theatre has become comfortable with the notion of *tragicomedy* to incorporate both genres. Tragicomedy allows practitioners to explore the seriousness of human experience without having to succumb to a final solution of death or banishment. Tragicomedy also seems more in line with current sensibilities that recognize some of the more dire circumstances of current society but maintain optimism about the human experience. Tom Stoppard's *Arcadia* is an example of a contemporary tragicomedy. The play relates the story of two scholars living in an English country house and their predecessors in the house 180 years prior. The witty dialogue elicits laughter, but the blending of the past and present invokes the tragic criteria of reversal of fortune and the fatal flaw. The play ends with both a waltz (comic celebration) and a contemplation of the end of the world.

Musical Theatre

Musical theatre is predominantly a form of entertainment that emerged from theatre in the United States. This is not to disassociate it from the grand tradition of European opera; however, here you are more likely to see a revival of Rodgers and Hammerstein than Richard Wagner or Amadeus Mozart. Like jazz, musical theatre has become one of the United States' most successful cultural exports. And much like the genres of comedy and tragedy, it is defined by the conventions of its form. These include reliance on spectacle and powerful music.

> It would be easy to assume that I am being critical of musical theatre because of its reliance on spectacle. On the contrary, I believe that musical theatre connects contemporary audiences with the fundamental nature of the theatre as a *theatron*, or "seeing place." I also believe that the popularity of musical theatre, particularly for American audiences, nurtures and sustains interest in the practice of theatre that could fall by the wayside among other entertainments.
>
> –Colleen Reilly

American musical theatre has its origins in **melodrama**, or musical drama. This was the predominant form of American stage entertainment in the 19th century. Melodrama is defined by its uncomplicated portrayal of good and evil through heroes and villains, exaggerated plotlines, and spectacular settings. Music underscored the action onstage and provoked an emotional response from the audience. American melodrama has eventually evolved into sitcoms and soap operas.

A few landmark musical theatre productions have come to inform the genre as it operates today. Among these is *Show Boat* (1927) by Jerome Kern and Oscar Hammerstein II. This production in many ways marks the advent of musical theatre as a form that seamlessly expresses plot, character, and thought through music, song, dialogue, and dance. Furthermore, it is one of the first stage productions to deal with racial tensions with its realistic depiction of African American levee workers and an interracial subplot. Other critical productions include *Oklahoma* (1943) by Richard Rodgers and Oscar Hammerstein II, which included a 15-minute dream ballet sequence; *Hair* (1967) by Galt MacDermot,

Gerome Ragni, and Joseph Rado, which concludes with an explosive audience inclusive celebration; and *Wicked* (2003) with Stephen Schwartz and Winnie Holman, which has broken box office records throughout the world. What ties each of these musicals together, and may be a testament to the American musical form, is that each of these promotes a message of tolerance and personal freedom.

Although the musicals mentioned earlier serve as examples of **book musicals**, or musicals where songs and dances are fully integrated into the storytelling, another form of musical theatre has emerged in the 20th century. It is largely based on the commercial demands of the Broadway theatre economy, but it also serves to energize and entertain contemporary audiences. The **jukebox musical** incorporates previously released music into the musical score. In some cases, these musicals are semi-biographical, and in others they provide a vehicle for popular music. Of these, *Mamma Mia* (1999) is perhaps the most well-known in its promotion of an ABBA soundtrack loosely linked around a contrived story.

Theatrical Styles

In addition to theatrical genre, it is important to consider the possibilities of theatrical style. Genre—tragedy, comedy, and musical theatre—is often determined by the dramatic text. The play that is being produced is often already composed as a particular genre. The fun for practitioners in theatre often comes from having a clear sense of stylistic choices that can be made that align with or against a particular dramatic text.

Realism

Late in the 19th century, stagecraft arrived at an opportunity to replicate life as the typical audience might experience it. This corresponded with the advent of photography and the fascination with documenting everyday experiences. Playwrights such as Henrik Ibsen became very interested in the behavior of everyday sort of people, and the style of **realism** began to dominate theatrical practice.

Take a minute and contemplate the paradox of theatrical realism. Theatre in its very nature is a practice of mimesis (imitation or representation). We do not want to fall into the trap that realism became the style that every subsequent style reacted against because at its heart, realism is the style most contradictory to theatrical practice.

Theatre cannot be realistic in the sense of depicting "reality" because it is constructed through an imaginary agreement between a practitioner, an action, a theatre, and an audience. Consequently, realism exists on a spectrum of numerous theatrical styles as a kind of metatheatrical game. The goals of 19th-century realism, to document everyday experience and behavior, have become subsumed by the camera technology that can accomplish such an objective. Contemporary theatrical realism has come to mean convincing an audience that the world that they see onstage is entirely possible in their own world. It maintains all of the conventions of our experiences, and does not allow theatricality (conventions, lights, sounds, costumes, etc.) to interrupt it.

Nonrealism

When we speak of **nonrealism** in the theatre, therefore, we speak of theatrical conventions that practitioners have constructed with specific goals in mind. Nonrealism in theatre is like the elements of style in visual arts. Brushstrokes that result in cubist or expressionistic paintings are deliberately used to achieve a particular result. Likewise, theatrical styles are used by practitioners to influence audience experiences and expectations. The styles listed in this chapter are by no means exhaustive; however, together with realism, they are likely to inform the theatre that you encounter here at Slippery Rock University and regional productions.

Historical Practices

Although it may seem counterintuitive, one of the trending contemporary styles is that of **historical practices**, that is, performing plays in the way that historical research suggests they may have been performed in their own time. This theatrical style came into vogue with the modern reconstruction of an architectural approximation of Shakespeare's Globe Theatre in London in 1997. This renewed interest in Shakespeare's theatrical conventions led to all-male productions of the plays under the artistic direction of Mark Rylance. Ongoing investigation of Shakespearean conventions has led to similar methodologies. The recent production of repertory productions using sides and textual cues for live interpretation of Shakespeare's plays for Laura Smiley's Unseam'd Shakespeare is a local example of this use of style. Similar incorporations of 17th- and 18th-century acting conventions inform contemporary productions that use historical practices.

Epic Theatre

One of the most influential practitioners of theatrical style in the 20th century is Bertolt Brecht (1898-1956). Brecht developed a form of theatre called **epic theatre**. Influenced by documentary techniques and the journalistic theatre of the 1930s when Living Newspapers were a primary way of communicating global news, epic theatre sought to pose a question about an issue that only the audience could resolve. Brecht wanted to continuously interrupt the theatrical illusion and remind the audience to be critical about the events that they witnessed onstage. He did this by using conventions that he referred to as "verfremdungseffekt" or "v-effect" or "alienation effect."

The "v-effect" devices were meant to jar the audience out of their natural sympathies for the characters and remain objective about the action. These devices might include announcing titles of scenes that contained the full action of the scene to eliminate suspense, including a song that contrasted the tone of the action with comedy or irony, insisting the actors report on the action rather than disappear into the constructed reality of a scene. By constantly reminding the audience that they were watching a performance, Brecht sought to prevent his audience from investing in the historical fiction he presented. Instead, he wanted the audience to contest the kind of narcotic entertainment they were accustomed to experience.

Theatre of Cruelty

Antonin Artaud (1896-1948) believed that the theatre was a place for ongoing spiritual practice. Like Brecht, he shied away from the idea that theatre should serve only to entertain an audience, and mined its possibilities to create extraordinary experiences. He recognized the special quality of creating a theatrical event in the presence of an audience. His intention was not to be "cruel" in the sense of being mean-spirited or vindictive, but instead to use theatre as a tool to confront truths in the world that an audience might not be expecting. The **theatre of cruelty** uses a kind of sensory overload of deconstructed language, the sound of musical instruments, and unconventional audience orientations. Artaud and his followers practiced this style of theatre out of a profound belief that theatre was the site for ritualistic practice.

Poor Theatre

Poor theatre is a style of theatre developed by Polish practitioner Jerzy Grotowski (1933-1999) in the 1960s. This method of production wanted to define the fundamental units of theatre and also wanted to strip away the invisible machinery of set, costume, and light changes. Instead, Grotowski wanted to immerse the audience in direct experience. In his landmark production of *Akropolis* by Stanislaw Wyspiański, his company of actors was dressed as concentration camp survivors. Throughout the course of the action of the play, the company constructed an enclosure around the audience that invoked the architecture of a crematorium. This radical treatment of the orientation of the audience and their experience has come to define the method of the poor theatre.

Grotowski later developed an interest in global theatre forms. He found the practice of theatre in non-Western nations to be revelatory in terms of the possibilities of the relationship between actors and audience, theatrical language, and ritual practice. Grotowski came to understand the role of theatre as a practice common to all human culture. He explored the possibilities of performance that explored common human expression and archetypal stories.

Theatre of the Oppressed

In 1974, Brazilian Augusto Boal published ***Theatre of the Oppressed***. Boal's main point is that all theatre, like all human activity, is political, and that it can be used as a weapon. Boal traces how theatre evolved in the time of the Greeks:

> "Theater" was the people singing freely in the open air; the theatrical performance was created by and for the people, and could thus be called dithyrambic song. It was a celebration in which all could participate freely. Then came the aristocracy and established divisions: some persons will go to the stage and only they will be able to act; the rest will remain seated, receptive, and passive—these will be the spectators, the masses, the people. And in order that the spectacle may efficiently reflect the dominant ideology, the aristocracy established another division: some actors will be protagonists (aristocrats) and the rest will be the chorus—symbolizing, in one way or another, the mass. (ix-x)[2]

---

[2]Boal, Augusto. *Theatre of the Oppressed.* Trans. Charles A. & María Odilia Leal McBride. New York: Theatre Communications Group, 1985. Print.

Boal then traces the development of Western theatre through the creation of psychologically realistic characters and Brecht's reaction to that, which was to take the characters and convert them into "an object of social forces, not of the values of the superstructures" (x).[3] *Theatre of the Oppressed*, then, takes the Brechtian idea and goes one step further: It breaks the barriers between actors and spectators, because "all must act, all must be protagonists in the necessary transformations of society....Thus we arrive at the *poetics of the oppressed*, the conquest of the means of theatrical production" (x).

Agitprop Theatre

Because Boal was educated, he published a book about his method of producing a people's theatre to promote social change. However, this method springs up spontaneously all over Latin America as the need for change pushes people to get creative with their methods of resisting oppression. One such case is the short-lived *Teatro de la Basura* (Trash Theatre), which was initiated by schoolteacher Candelario Reyes in Northern Honduras in the late 1980s as a method for rehearsing possible ways that *campesinos* (subsistence farmers) could resist the oppression and power of the landowners. Farmers who had lived in one area for generations (before the Spanish came to the Americas) suddenly found that some rich person had "bought" the land they were farming (they held no title because the indigenous came from a truly paperless society). These farmers worked all day in the fields, and then rehearsed and created plays about their situation, including various ways of confronting the landowners about the violence that their hired private armies carried out against them.

There were several "Theatre for Peace" festivals until they finally ran out of funding to carry on the activity. I participated in one such festival, and was impressed at the quality of acting and the treatment of serious social problems. All plays were followed by talk-backs between the actors and the audience members, in which anyone could respectfully offer advice, suggestions, and criticism of the theme and performance.

–Deb Cohen

This style of theatre appears not only in Latin America, but in the United States as well. In 1965 in California, the Teatro Campesino was founded to further the cause of the United Farm Workers. Chicano Luis Valdez, a founding member of this movement, has become one of the most influential performance artists in American history. Likewise, the 1960s saw the establishment of the Bread and Puppet Theatre in Vermont. This puppet-based agitprop performance troupe serves bread to its audience at every performance to heighten the communion between the performance and its participants.

---

[3]Boal, Augusto. *Theatre of the Oppressed*. Trans. Charles A. & María Odilia Leal McBride. New York: Theatre Communications Group, 1985. Print.

Devised Theatre

Devised theatre is unusual in that it does not originate with a single dramatic text. Instead, practitioners collaborate around an idea or event. The rehearsal process is often marked by exploration and improvisation that then become transposed into a working theatrical draft. Working collaboratively or under single direction, devised theatre often poetically illustrates the numerous viewpoints that surround a particular issue. One example would be the work of Complicite, a British theatre company devoted to the devised method since 1983. Perhaps most telling of this company and the process is the way that they designate their collaborators as Performers, Creatives, and Production. Individuals in each of these areas contribute to the devised process as they are needed, and the result it a style of theatre that is driven by the actor's craft and creative vision.

COSTA RICAN GROUP TIERRANEGRA ["BLACK EARTH"] AND THEIR PLAY, *THE INVASION* (1973)
Eugenia Chaverri, one of the founders of Tierranegra, wrote about her experience as a Preface to the publication of the play to commemorate its 30th anniversary in 2003. She relates that the process had three stages: First was to choose the invasions the play would cover. Next, group members researched these invasions, including copying important speeches or other documents (primarily the novels *Más Abajo de la Piel* ["Beneath the Skin"] by Abel Pacheco and *Mamita Yunai* [a reference to the United Fruit Company] by Carlos Luis Fallas) to be incorporated into the dialogue. Finally, one member took charge of directing the improvisations and consolidating the play's design and text.

The play begins in a classroom, with the teacher reviewing a history lesson about American William Walker's invasion of Nicaragua in 1855 and Costa Rica's armed response to his threat as he approached the Costa Rican border. Through dialogue, song, and dance, the group re-creates the three key historical invasions: the Spanish Conquest of the Americas in the 1500s; the formation of modern Costa Rica (the battle of Ochomogo, in which San José became the capital city, is played out as a soccer match) and Walker's attempt to take over Central America in the 1800s; and finally, the capitalist invasion of the transnational American banana companies in the 1930s.

–Deb Cohen

Improvisation/Solo Performance

One of the most accessible and enduring forms of theatrical style is **improvisation**. At its center, improvisational theatre is based on a social contract between actors and audience to believe in imaginary circumstances. In an improvisational scene, an actor must give as many details using language and mime. Working with other actors, they must agree to any given circumstances that the imaginary scene requires. This is often referred to as the "yes, and..." technique. One actor makes a suggestion. The second actor must agree to whatever that premise might be and immediately provide further details about the setting, their relationship, and any impending circumstances. In the United States, improvisational theatre is primarily used for comedy.

Chitlin' Circuit

The **Chitlin' Circuit** is one of the most powerful commercial forces in contemporary theatre. It has a long history with theatrical practice in the United States and survives as the remnants of theatrical spaces throughout the Southeast and Eastern seaboards that have been friendly to African American performers dating back to the 19th century. The Chitlin' Circuit serves a kind of bridge between popular entertainment and what we perceive to be legitimate theatre. Actor, director, and producer Tyler Perry has extensively discussed the role of the Chitlin' Circuit in African American theatrical presentation, and acknowledges its role in his extraordinary success.

Spanish Language Theatre in the United States

Some Spanish-speaking theatre companies predate the existence of the United States, because states in the Southwest were originally part of Mexico. Although English-speaking theatre practitioners are generally formed in university theatre departments throughout the country, Spanish-speakers may train in Miami's Teatro Prometeo [Prometheus Theatre], whose "2-year Professional Actor Training Program is unique in the nation offering the opportunity of conservatory-style actor training in Spanish."[4] Spanish-language theatre thrives in the Southwest, as well as in the Chicago area, Washington, D.C., Florida, and New York.

Conclusion

Theatrical genre and theatrical style have a tremendous impact on the choices that all practitioners make in preparation for theatrical production. Although genre often applies most directly to the play or text being considered for production, theatrical style can radically enhance, alter, or enlighten the treatment of that text. As theatrical conventions dictated by genre and style become more familiar to an audience, the theatrical experience can likewise by heightened.

Works Cited

Mercier, Vivian. *Irish Times*, 18 February 1956.
Miller, Arthur. *Death of a Salesman*. New York: Penguin, 1996.

[4]http://www.prometeotheatre.com/english/eng_history.htm

Suggested Exercise

The class will select a familiar story to complete the exercise. The *Three Little Pigs* is a good candidate because the action is simple and repetitive. Working in small groups, create an outline of three to five scenes that are crucial for the story. Complete the following questions:

1. Which genre do you feel your action most resembles? Comedy? Tragedy? Musical Theatre?
2. Of your scenes, designate at least one that will be realized through the style of "realism." Describe it in paragraph form. What does the audience see? What is the language like? How does the audience feel?
3. Of your scenes, designate two to three that will be realized through alternative styles: EPIC THEATRE, IMPROVISATION, POOR THEATRE, THEATRE OF THE OPPRESSED, DEVISED THEATRE, AGITPROP, THEATRE OF CRUELTY, or HISTORICAL PRACTICES. Describe these in paragraph form. What does the audience see? What is the language like? How does the audience feel?
4. Reflect on the exercise in a 1-minute paper. How do genre and style contribute to theatrical choices? Which of these do you find interesting? Which of these do you find least interesting? Why or why not?

GLOBAL THEATRICAL FORMS
Rebecca Morrice and Deb Cohen

13

CHAPTER OBJECTIVES
- Describe a variety of styles of theatre from Japan, China, India, Africa, and Latin America.
- Explain the origins of shadow puppet theatre.
- Explain the cultural background and significance of these styles of theatre.

KEY TERMS

Convention
Griot
Hanamichi
Hashigakari
Hurry door
Joruri
Kora
Mie
Onnagata
Shamisen
Verbal scene painting

Much of what has been written in this textbook focuses on the styles of theater that are most familiar to the majority of our students—that of North America and Europe. It would be unfair, however, to leave you with the impression that theater is the same all over the world when, in fact, it has developed in very different ways in other countries.

This chapter is designed to give you a brief overview of some of the most well-known styles of theatre from around the world, but it is by no means exhaustive. There are more styles of theatre performance throughout the world than could ever be covered in an introductory text. It is only hoped that this chapter will expand your ideas and thoughts about what theatre actually *is*, not just what it is in the United States and Europe.

Latin American Theatre

Theatrical performances have been in existence in many places in Latin America since the development of civilizations there. However, only a few pre-Columbian plays still exist and/or are performed regularly: the *Rabinal Achí* of the Maya in Guatemala, and *Ollantay*, the historical Incan drama from Peru. In Mexico, many predominantly indigenous towns recreate the Spanish Conquest in performances that involve the entire population and can last several days.

Serious literary study of Latin American theatre (as opposed to superficial newspaper reviews) dates back to the 1940s, according to *A Bibliography of Latin American Theater Criticism*. In the United States, Frank Dauster (Rutgers), Leon Lyday (Penn State), and George Woodyard (University of Kansas) pioneered the study of Latin American theatre in the 1960s, and created the first academic programs in the new discipline. Woodyard also founded the *Latin American Theatre Review*, an academic journal that is nearing its 50th anniversary.

With all this academic study, why don't Americans know Latin American theatre as well as they know its novels or poetry? The answer is pretty straightforward: logistics (distribution) and the language barrier. Just as in the United States, not much theatre is published in comparison with novels and nonfiction in Latin America. In addition, it is much easier and more common for a Latin American to know and purchase an American or European play than one written in a neighboring country. Furthermore, because the market is so small for theatre in the first place, those few Latin American plays that are translated rarely become published and distributed in the United States. Finally, because so few plays and histories of Latin American theatre are available in English, most theatre curricula in the United States do not address this region at all.

Most theatre practitioners in Latin America learn about what people in other places are doing via regional or international theatre festivals, like the huge one in Bogotá, Colombia, where in 2012, in addition to the 60 Colombian theatre companies present, there were 65 international companies from 35 countries represented. Another important festival is *Mayo Teatral* ("Theatre in May"), a festival sponsored by the Casa de las Americas in even years since the 1960s in Havana, Cuba. Some theatre scholars and practitioners travel illegally to Cuba to attend this event.

LATIN AMERICAN THEATRE AND SRU

Deb Cohen (Modern Languages and Cultures) presented the first Latin American play in English translation in 2000. *Only You*, a play about two Mexican brothers that covered important socio-historical events from the 1960s to the 1990s, played to standing room audiences in Sheehy Theatre. In 2003, Cohen mounted a staged reading of her English translation of *Chapulines and Other Critters* by Costa Rican Walter Fernández. In 2007, theatre students from 100 level Spanish classes presented "The Man Who Turned into a Dog," by Argentine Osvaldo Dragún. Most recently, Laura Smiley agreed to direct Cohen's translation of Costa Rican Melvin Méndez's play, *The Old Man's Wings*. The play revolves around an old man and his attempts to leave the institution for the mentally disabled so that he can return to his normal life. Antonio, the old man, was found catatonic following the accidental drowning of his daughter. His nurse, Elena, lets him work on a pair of wings as occupational therapy, but the old man actually manages to fly away with them. Upon his return, he enlists the help of the other inmates to fly back with him and stop a dam project that threatens to drown his home village, just as his daughter drowned.

The antagonist of the play is the Director of the institution, a stodgy but lecherous doctor, who prefers to drug his patients to keep them quiet and manageable, rather than to really treat their problems. After Antonio's return, he warns Elena of the chaos that Antonio can provoke among the others with his wild ideas and false hopes. Elena's reply is the heart of the play, which takes themes of madness and sanity from *Don Quijote de la Mancha* and mixes it with an ecological message about the price of industrial progress on the environment and the people living in the way of progress.

ELENA: Chaos, Doctor? Chaos because he looks at others and reminds them that it's possible to smile...Chaos, because he is willing to chat with anybody about his life without fear, because he accepts us unconditionally? Chaos, because he planted the seeds of a dream in everybody? Chaos, because he wants to fight for his village so they don't remove all traces of his past....Chaos because he believes in something, and learned to fly? (*pause*) I'd like a little piece of that chaos for myself, Doctor!

In the end, Antonio submits to the Doctor's forced medication, and Elena builds herself a pair of wings and flies back to the dam to prevent its opening.

Photo courtesy of Michael Boone.

Japanese Theatre

Although there is a fair amount of modern and avant-garde theatre being created in Japan, for our purposes here, we are going to study three forms that have deep roots in the Japanese culture, stretching back several centuries. The three classical forms of theatre in Japan that we will survey are Bunraku, Kabuki, and Noh (No), each of which has a very distinctive style and approach. They are all at least 400 years old, whereas the oldest, Noh, can be traced back to the 14th century.

Noh

Noh, which literally means "skill," was originally developed as an entertainment for the Japanese shogun and his court, and in its efforts to combine the Zen principles of restraint and simplicity, is more elegant and refined than the entertainments for the commoners. Its Zen Buddhist influences and intentionally slow, deliberate pace were meant to inspire thought and contemplativeness in the audience. Noh performers have historically been all male, and the acting profession has traditionally been a hereditary one, passed down from father to son.

In a typical Noh performance, many of the performers wear masks that are smaller than the actors' own face, and much focus is put into stylized movements and a deliberate style of walking. In European theatre, the focus is often on the actor's face, but here, there is more importance given to the full-body movement of the actor, and each gesture has meaning and significance.

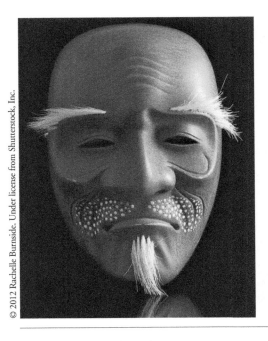
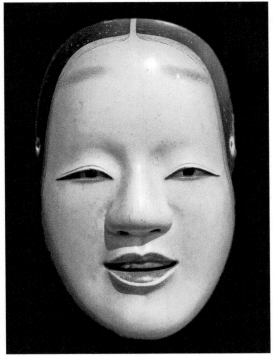

© 2012 Rachelle Burnside. Under license from Shutterstock, Inc.

© 2012 Fedor Selivanov. Under license from Shutterstock, Inc.

Typical Japanese Noh masks.

© Robbie Jack/Corbis

Waki-Jun Mucase performs in a Umewaka Kennokai Noh Theatre production of "Aoi No Ue."

Originally, Noh performances took place in outdoor garden shrines. When the performances moved indoors and the tradition of Noh was standardized in the 1600s, the stage retained the look of the shrines with the roofed areas of the *butai* (main performance area) and the **hashigakari** (the bridge that the actors enter upon). The pillars that support the stage roofs are used by the actors not only to help orient themselves while their faces are covered by masks, but also have a performance function. The main character typically enters and pauses at the upstage right pillar while he tells the audience his name and where he comes from. He looks at the "gazing" pillar downstage right while he makes this announcement. The secondary character is associated with the downstage left pillar while the flute player commonly found in Noh performances stands at the upstage left pillar.

The performers are accompanied by a small chorus that provides additional narration and singing. Whereas the main characters will make their entrances and exits along the *hashigakari*, a second entrance, called the **hurry door** is used by the chorus and stage assistants. The hurry door is typically only 3-feet tall and forces the people using it to enter and exit in a bowed position, highlighting their hierarchically lesser role in the performance.

The costumes for Noh actors are based on the fashions popular in the 14th century and are very stylized with even the patterns on the layers of kimono being indicative to the audience. For instance, a kimono covered in a hexagonal pattern might represent a thunder god, whereas a kimono covered in triangles might tell the audience that the character is representing a serpent.

Noh plays are divided into several different types. There are plays about women, warriors, people who are mentally deranged because of a terrible event in their lives, spirits, demons, and plays that honor the gods. Originally, Noh performances would consist of five different plays being presented in one program. In modern times, that has been cut down to two or three.

Kabuki

Although Noh was created and designed to entertain a higher class, more refined audience, Kabuki began as a common entertainment for everyone. First started in 1603 by a female dancer, Kabuki changed significantly in 1629 and again in 1652 when the government stepped in and banned females and young males from performing after fears of immorality became widespread. This led to Kabuki being performed solely by men with many of the traditions being passed from father to son, as with Noh. This meant that all the roles, even the female characters, were portrayed by men. Actors who perfected and specialized in the performance of female roles in Kabuki are called **onnagata**.

Kabuki performances are more fast-paced than Noh and often contain elements of special effects and acrobatics, with elevator traps and revolving stages being commonly used by the early 18th century. The stage for a Kabuki performance bears some resemblance to that used for Noh, but one significant difference allows the performers much more connection to the actors. The bridge that the primary characters make their entrances on, in this case, called the **hanamichi**, comes directly through the audience. Kabuki audiences are not shy about shouting out their support for their favorite actors as they make their grand entrances.

Kabuki performances already had a long tradition of combining bold makeup, colorful costumes, and popular stories, especially of urban life and samurai, but eventually began adding additional elements to keep pace with audience demands and expectations. Once the popular puppet theatre, Bunraku, had become well established, the Kabuki actors began performing **mie**, which are moments in a Kabuki performance when an actor will begin to move in a very wooden, puppet-like way and then strike a frozen pose. This is all done to enhance a particularly meaningful moment in the action and was quite popular with the audiences. Eventually, acrobatics, live musicians, narrators, and scenic elements such as trap doors, stage elevators, and revolving floors were added, all to keep Kabuki one of the most diversely entertaining types of theatre.

A Japanese Kabuki performer.

Bunraku

Of all the types of traditional Japanese theatre, Bunraku is perhaps the one that is most unusual to a Western audience member. A type of puppet theatre begun in the 17th century, Bunraku has enjoyed immense popularity throughout much of its history, but not as a children's entertainment. Instead, Bunraku was meant to be enjoyed by audiences of all ages, and the puppets are individually handcrafted works of art. Each puppet, which is roughly two-thirds life size (3-4 feet tall) is controlled by three men. The main puppeteer controls the head and the right arm of the puppet, whereas his two assistants control the feet (or hem of the skirt of a legless female puppet) and the left arm. The

A Japanese Bunraku puppet and master puppeteer.

master puppeteer is traditionally the only one whose face is allowed to be seen by the audience; the two assistants wear black robes and hoods to cover their faces. This **convention** is known by the audience to mean that these two puppeteers are essentially invisible. Allowing the main puppeteer's face to be seen by the audience is a measure of respect paid to the individual onstage who is recognized as the master. Respect is a very important part of Japanese culture, and this practice follows the practice of recognizing those accomplished artists, some of whom are considered "national treasures."

Bunraku performances are accompanied not only by musicians who underscore the action of the play, but also by narrators (**joruri**) who provide the voices for the puppets. The puppeteers do not speak for the puppets; this would be considered distracting and undignified. Typical instruments used by the musicians include the classical **shamisen**, a stringed instrument similar to a guitar with a very distinctive sound.

Many plays written for Bunraku are derived from a popular tale called the *Chushingura*. Also known as the Tale of the 47 Samurai, the story is based on an actual event in which a group of sumarai who, after avenging a grievous wrong done to their master, commit mass suicide. This tale was immensely popular and was eventually the basis for dozens of Bunraku and Kabuki plays.

Chinese Theatre

Some of the earliest forms of Chinese theatre are known to have existed as early as the second century C.E., and throughout its long history many different forms have existed—some created by the ruling dynasties, some by the lower classes.

Music, colorful costumes, and acrobatics have been common to many of these forms, but the one form that survives and has come to be recognized as China's "national theatre" is the Beijing Opera (also known as the Peking Opera).

Beijing Opera

The one form of classical Chinese theatre that we will explore is the Beijing Opera (also called the Peking Opera), which was the dominant form of theatre beginning around the mid-1800s. The focus in this type of theatre is an entertainment that blends elements of acting, dancing, singing, and acrobatics. There are both male and female actors, and they all go through very vigorous training to prepare for the acrobatic swordplay and dancing typically seen in this form of theatre. Many performers begin training as young children and spend their lives in the profession.

Actress of the Beijing Opera Troupe performs the famous story "Journey to the West."

In addition to the scripted portions of the acts or plays, the actors are also allowed to improvise portions of the performance. Stories about good versus evil

Actors of the Beijing Opera Troupe perform the famous story "Journey to the West."

© 2012 Hung Chung Chih . Under license from Shutterstock, Inc.

are common, and female warriors are particularly well-loved by audiences. Unlike with traditional forms of Japanese theatre, women are allowed to perform in Beijing Opera, but as a nation under close governmental control, the subject matter of performances is nearly always from the distant past. For fear of presenting subject matter that could inspire antigovernment sentiment, Beijing Opera performances avoid modern events and conflict. No matter the theme or events in the play, all performances of Beijing Opera end happily.

Theatre of India

Much of what we know today about the theatrical traditions in India is owed to the existence of a book called *Natyasastra* ("The Art of Theatre"). The exact date of its writing is debated, but many scholars place it around the second century C.E., and it is the most extensive historical documentation of any form of world theatre. Of the forms described in the *Natyasastra*, perhaps the most important to explore is Sanskrit theatre. Although extinct now, many other forms of Indian theatre grew out of the traditions of Sanskrit.

At its core, Sanksrit theatre was a form that combined stylized vocal patterns, hand gestures (pantomime), dance, and costumes to tell stories most often based in the spiritual and emotional lives of its characters rather than on their realistic existence. The earliest plays are dated around the second century C.E. and are often based on Indian mythology. Each play was dominated by a primary emotion or state (e.g., erotic, comic, heroic, offensive, fear, sorrow) and was always about the issue of "right versus wrong," with "right" always winning. Very little scenery was used, but the makeup and costumes were very

Martin Harvey/Getty Images

Kathakali performer in a traditional costume.

© Will Gray/JAI/Corbis

One of the styles of makeup and costume common to Kathakali.

elaborate. Plays could typically run 6 hours long, and death and violence were not allowed to occur in front of the audience. Elaborate hand gestures; eye, neck, and brow movements; and various leaps and styles of walking, all put together much like a style of sign language, were utilized to help tell the story to the audience.

Kathakali

One of the forms of classical Indian Theatre that developed from Sanskrit drama and is still performed today is Kathakali, which is also a form of "dance theatre." Sometimes also referred to as "story play," Kathakali, which dates back to the 17th century, relies on dance and more than 600 separate gestures to tell a story. Many plays are derived from two of India's most famous epics: the *Mahabharata* (*Great Battle of the Bharata Family*) and *Ramayana* (*The Journey of Rama*). These tales are similar to *The Iliad* and *The Odyssey* in their respective places in literature and have served as the basis of a large number of plays in the Indian culture.

Kathakali performers typically train for a minimum of 6 to 10 years and begin training around age 10, with extreme flexibility and a widely expressive face being key areas of focus. They are accompanied onstage by a drummer and two singers whose lyrics, combined with the actors' expressions and gestures, tell the story to the audience.

Performances of Kathakali are typically full plays or a combination of scenes pulled from various plays tied together by a common theme. They are sometimes performed though the night, beginning as night starts and ending as the sun rises in the morning. This is done to make a symbolic connection with the good characters prevailing over evil by the end of the play (and the rising of the sun).

Theatre Of Islam

Islam is a common religion in many Middle East countries and in parts of Eastern Europe and Asia, including parts of Spain, Egypt, and Africa. Within the Koran, which is the Islamic equivalent to the Bible, it is made clear that the use of "graven images" is forbidden, which resulted in the development of the arts, including theatre, taking a different approach than in other cultures. Although there are still cultures of storytelling and performance in most Islamic countries, in some where the interpretation of "graven image" is more fundamental, performers had to get creative to get around the rule, which essentially forbids actors to perform directly in front of an audience. Cleverly, the use of shadow puppets became one solution to this challenge.

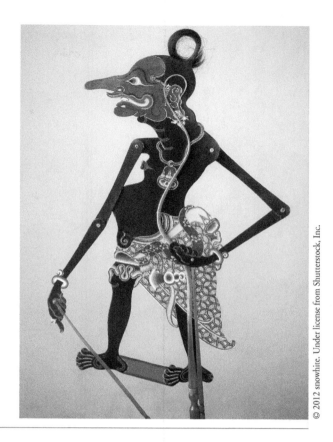

Two different styles of shadow puppets.

Shadow Puppets

The first known shadow puppets may have been used in China as early as the first century B.C.E. In Turkey, the puppet theatre is known as Karagoz and is believed to have been introduced in the 13th century C.E. Traditionally, a shadow puppet performance is presented to the audience using flat puppets, often made of leather or thick paper on sticks, that are placed in between a beam of light and a piece of cloth. The shadows that are created in the shape of the puppets allow the audience to enjoy the telling of a story without fear of looking upon a "graven image" because the shadow is not the object itself.

In some countries where the religion is or has been more fundamental, the puppets never evolved beyond more than a crudely cut out piece of leather. In other cultures where the religion was less strict, the puppets became more elaborate, even sometimes having pieces of colored vellum, which allowed for colors to be present in the shadows on the cloth. In still other cultures, the puppets were articulated, meaning that their joints were moveable, which created more lifelike movement by the puppets.

In any case, it is a positive statement regarding the need for and power of theatre within a culture that, despite so many obstacles that kept traditional live theatre from being presented, people still found away to share their stories through theatre.

Griots from Mali, Africa.

African Theatre

Given the size of the continent of Africa and the large number of cultures that have been a part of its history, it would be impossible to even begin a real survey of the different styles of theatre that have evolved there. However, one style of performance can be found in common within many of the cultures of Africa, especially those of western Africa, and that is the tradition of the **griot**.

Griot

Popular throughout many of the countries of western Africa for centuries, the griot tradition combines a mixture of storytelling, history, poetry, mime, singing, and dancing to entertain the audience; it dates back to the 14th century. Griots are commonly wandering performers and are more likely to be found entertaining a group of people on a sidewalk than on a stage. Audience members commonly sing along, and the performance can become quite interactive when an audience becomes fully involved. Griot performances tend to blend not only stories from the past but also modern current events, and through wit and satirical humor, they can often rouse an audience to quite a boisterous level.

As a wandering performer, a griot often has little to enhance his performance other than his own voice, sense of humor, and a traditional 21-stringed instrument known as a **kora**. Because they generally have no scenery and are often performing outside, griot also typically make wide use of a technique called **verbal scene painting**. The following excerpt from Shakespeare's play *The Tempest* is an example of this technique, which helps the audience see in their imagination the setting needed for the performance.

PROSPERO:
Ye elves of hills, brooks, standing lakes, and groves;
And ye that on the sands with printless foot
Do chase the ebbing Neptune, and do fly him
When he comes back; you demi-puppets that
By moonshine do the green sour ringlets make
Whereof the ewe not bites; and you whose pastime
Is to make midnight mushrooms, that rejoice
To hear the solemn curfew; by whose aid,—
Weak masters though ye be,—I have bedimm'd
The noontide sun, call'd forth the mutinous winds,

> And 'twixt the green sea and the azur'd vault
> Set roaring war: to the dread rattling thunder
> Have I given fire, and rifted Jove's stout oak
> With his own bolt: the strong-bas'd promontory
> Have I made shake; and by the spurs pluck'd up
> The pine and cedar

The goal with writing of this type is to evoke for the audience a setting that might not be possible with actual scenery. The audience's imagination is enough to transport them to the magical place Prospero describes. This is a technique that has long been used by writers, poets, and storytellers who have not always had the benefit of elaborate scenic effects. Through their incomparable performance style, the African griots use this technique to conjure exotic locations and other locales for their viewers.

Conclusion

In nearly every culture, either modern or from the past, there is evidence of a theatrical tradition existing within it. It seems that human beings have always been compelled to act and perform, whether it be to entertain, educate, pass on tradition, or provoke, but it is intriguing to see the countless different forms that it has taken. Although for many people living in the Western Hemisphere today theatre is primarily a form of entertainment performed in a proscenium-style theatre, this chapter shows that this particular style of theatre is relatively new in form and not what you might normally see in a different country. Knowing about these styles of theatre allows practitioners to expand their imaginations in an ongoing effort to please and entertain their audiences, and allows audiences a wider global perspective on what, historically and culturally, has been called "theatre."

Suggested Exercise

- Research and re-create an element from one of these styles of theatre (i.e., a mask, shadow puppet, costume, set piece).
- Research and re-create one of these elements of performance (i.e., Kathakali gestures, mie poses, shadow puppet performance).